PAVED WITH GOOD INTENTIONS: BACKGROUND TO THE GATT, URUGUAY ROUND AND WTO

Edited by

Yash Tandon & Megan Allardice

SEATINI
20 Victoria Drive
Newlands
Harare
Zimbabwe

Printed by Skilled Press P/L
119 Nelson Mandela Avenue
Harare
Zimbabwe

ISBN 0-7974-2712-0

TABLE OF CONTENTS

NOTES ON THE CONTRIBUTORS

MEGAN ALLARDICE is a freelance consultant based in Harare Zimbabwe. She has worked with SEATINI on the Institute's 'Strengthening Africa in World Trade' series of workshops and on its publications programme.

BHAGIRATH LAL DAS is the former Indian Ambassador and Permanent Representative to GATT and also former Director of International Trade Programmes in UNCTAD.

MILES KAHLER is a specialist in international relations and international political economy at the University of California San Diego, a member of the editorial board of *International Organization* and was Senior Fellow in International Political Economy at the Council on Foreign Relations.

JOHN ODELL is a Professor in the School of International Relations, University of Southern California and a former Editor of *International Organization*. He has conducted research in Asia, Latin America and Europe for the WTO and the IMF.

CHANDRAKANT PATEL was a senior official at UNCTAD gaining experience of LDC programmes and technical assistance activities. He is currently SEATINI's representative in Geneva and represented SEATINI at the Doha Ministerial meeting.

CHAKRAVARTHI RAGHAVAN is the founder and Chief Editor of the Geneva based *South-North Development Monitor* (SUNS) and has been a commentator of GATT and World Trade issues since 1980. He is also Editor of the fortnightly magazine *Third World Economics*, published by the Third World Network.

VINOD REGE is a retired senior official of the GATT Secretariat and is currently a consultant in the Commonwealth Secretariat.

MAGDA SHAHIN is a Minister Plenipotentiary of the Mission of Egypt to the WTO. She was one of the leading negotiators in the Committee on Trade and Environment of the WTO in the negotiations in preparation for the first WTO Ministerial Conference held in Singapore in December 1996.

YASH TANDON is the Director of the Southern and Eastern African Trade, Information and Negotiations Institute (SEATINI), based in Harare Zimbabwe. He has represented both Zimbabwe and Uganda at Ministerial Conferences of the WTO.

THE UNITED NATIONS CONFERENCE ON TRADE AND DEVELOPMENT (UNCTAD) established in 1964, aims to integrate developing countries into the world economy in a development friendly manner. UNCTAD is the focal point within the United Nations for the integrated treatment of trade and development, and the related issues of finance, technology, investment and sustainable development.

PREFACE

For many years, it has been apparent that the multilateral trading system provides little benefit to the countries of the south. Despite 'assistance' from the World Bank and the International Monetary Fund (IMF), and so called equal membership of the World Trade Organisation (WTO), the south has grown poorer, while the countries of the north continue to grow richer.

This is not surprising because the international trading and financial systems are merely extras in the service of the new 'global empire' (the alliance between Britain and the US), which is trying to enforce its dominance over world geopolitical structures, trade and finance, in the wake of the end of the cold war and the attack on the World Trade Centre on 11 September 2000. The April 2003 invasion of Iraq revealed the final part of the US/UK master plan - to control world politics through the unremitting, and only thinly justified, use of armed intervention. A crucial aspect of this control lies in ensuring that the US dollar continues to underpin world currencies at a time when its supremacy is threatened by the increasing crisis of international capitalism. It is no coincidence that when Saddam Hussein challenged the empire by demanding that Iraq's oil be denominated not in US dollars but in Euros, while at the same time handing over oil concessions to France and Russia, America and Britain felt compelled to invade Iraq.

But while the US and Britain compete with Europe and Japan for the world's resources and markets, these two groups will also collude with each other to defend and promote their collective interests in the global system. In this battle the WTO is a critical tool, opening up developing country markets, weakening their governments' regulatory powers and ensuring that the big capital of transnational corporations (TNCs) can move freely. The reality of international trading arrangements, then, is that they have been established by the north, using their rules and standards, to create a system to further enrich the north and ensure captive markets and sources of raw materials in the south.

The WTO's objectives are benignly stated as helping producers of goods and services, exporters, and importers conduct their business. The Organisation also claims to be 'democratic', 'member driven' and 'rules based', and to give all member states an equal voice. But, it has become clear that some states are more equal than others. Since the end of the cold war, the US has been striving unceasingly for world domination and the huge business conglomerates which have such inordinate power over the 'democratic' process in the US, have had no hesitation in ensuring that the WTO is used to further their trading and profit interests. Furthermore, the entire neoliberal economic agenda teeters on the brink of crises for which it has no explanations and, more dangerously, only short term solutions. It is this cliff edge state that has seen world capital relying increasingly on speculative activities and less and less on production. It makes inevitable the growing chasm between the rich and the poor, both within and among nations. For big business has no other answer to its inherent crises than to export them to those countries which cannot fight back. This is the function for which the WTO has been commandeered.

The structural adjustment programmes that many developing countries were forced to adopt under the Empire's other wing, the Bretton Woods Institutions, have included the liberalisation of their capital accounts, leaving them without protection against currency speculators and other raiders.

Over the period since the WTO was formed, increases in trade volume have largely been among the quad countries (the USA, Europe, Canada and Japan), leaving the developing countries, and Africa in particular, more and more marginalised and vulnerable. Even more than powerful countries and blocs, globalisation benefits TNCs, allowing them increasing freedom to move capital across borders, to invest (and to withdraw investment) in pursuit of their own advantage, ignoring local conditions and legislation.

It is this last aspect of the global system that has been most successfully disguised under the mountains of negotiation and educational literature regarding the various multilateral trade agreements. Trade is, and has always been, for profit - the profit of the investor. Any side benefits arising for the local community in which the investor operates, are just that, side benefits, not part of the intended outcome. Unfortunately the UN and those bodies which were established to ensure benefit to the developing world have also been hijacked to serve the new empire's interests. As a result, their perspectives have changed significantly over the past few years. All these agencies now subscribe to and promote the unproven notion that economic growth will inevitably lead to development in the south, through the 'trickle down' mechanism. Thus the future of development has been made hostage to the benevolence of the 'free' market.

Neoliberal economics, the ideology which is used to window dress the empire's naked demands, argues that markets benefit consumers, denying the more obvious truth that they serve the suppliers. Consumers benefit only when it is in the producers' interests that they should do so. 'Free trade' is a myth perpetuated in the service of the empire's goals. The empire's view of democracy finds its clearest expression in the operations of the WTO, where member countries are differentially 'equal' and where 'consensus' is claimed in absentia and in the midst of guided ignorance. The history of the negotiations has been one in which the rich countries boldly pursue their own interests, while paying lip service to the needs of the developing countries.

The pressure by American pharmaceutical companies within the multilateral trading system was already evident in 1994 with the Uruguay Round negotiations of the GATT. Despite the protests of the developing countries, the Trade Related aspects of Intellectual Property Rights (TRIPS) Agreement was introduced. Since then, in the countries of the north, the line between big business and politicians has grown ever less distinct and the WTO is becoming the international arbiter of matters which should rightly be the responsibility of national governments and their legislators.

The Southern and Eastern African Trade Information and Negotiations Institute (SEATINI) was formed in response to the clearly inequitable processes observed at the 1997 Singapore WTO Ministerial Conference. Developing countries, especially those from Africa, found themselves isolated, neither understanding the processes and their implications, nor having the capacity in terms of skills, experience and personnel, to negotiate as equal partners with their developed country 'partners'.

The WTO provides functional training for third world negotiators; in other words training that makes them more compliant to the needs of the stronger countries and the TNCs, and less able to pursue their own countries' interests. SEATINI seeks to strengthen the role of Southern and Eastern African countries and more broadly, other African and developing countries, in the multilateral trading system. It does this by holding capacity building workshops for trade negotiators, workshops around specific trade issues for other interested groups, such as parliamentarians and the media, and by disseminating information through its fortnightly bulletin and other publications. SEATINI was formed under the auspices of the International South Group Network (ISGN), a south-south network that challenges the process of globalisation and its assumptions, and recognises the need for alternative modes of development.

SEATINI, along with other NGOs fighting on the same front, can claim some degree of success in this work, given the responses of developing country negotiators subsequent to Singapore. Africa now puts forward its own, frequently well informed, position papers in advance of statements from the WTO Secretariat, examples being the case of TRIPs and the issue of seed patents, and on market access for non-agricultural goods.

The Readings in Globalisation and World Trade series covers a broad range of themes around the phenomenon of globalisation and a number of specific trade issues. The intention is to examine and expose the realities of the multilateral trading system and globalisation from a southern perspective. Many of the pieces used in each of the volumes in the series were generated under the auspices of SEATINI's activities. It is hoped that their wider dissemination through this series will increase the level of discussion of these issues and provide a warning to those tempted to take the WTO and other institutions of globalisation at face value.

INTRODUCTION

Megan Allardice

The General Agreement on Tariffs and Trade (GATT) was set up as a provisional agreement in 1947, on the basis of the 1946 Havana Charter, to replace the bilateral trade diplomacy, agreements and conflicts that had marked the period between the First and Second World Wars, with a multilateral system. The vision of the Havana Charter was the formation of a multilateral trading body (originally dubbed the ITO) which would be to world trade what the recently conceived IMF and World Bank were to international finance. However, protectionist interests quickly came into play with the United States, a signatory to the GATT, refusing to ratify it for fear of the negative effects on domestic industry that would arise from the opening up of its own markets.

Thus, the GATT existed for 47 years as a provisional treaty and arrangement, operating under a 'secretariat' led by an 'executive secretary' who only adopted the more grandiose title of 'Director General' in 1963 (Rhaghavan, p9 this volume). The negotiation of the Havana Charter, dealing as it did with situations obtaining before and after the Second World War, took place among those countries most directly involved in the War, the United States, Japan, Britain and Western Europe. It comprised a series of agreements on different areas of international trade which the contracting parties signed on an agreement-by-agreement basis. On the same basis, various of the developing nations signed onto one or other of the agreements as the need arose.

It was not until the beginning of 1995 that the World Trade Organisation came into existence, operationalising the Marrakesh Agreement of 1994 and the version of GATT appended thereto. The Marrakesh Agreement was the conclusion of the Uruguay Round of multilateral trade negotiations launched, officially, in 1986. However, it is now clear that manouvering and 'pre-negotiation' had taken place for a few years before 1986 amongst those who held, and desired to maintain, power and strategic advantage within the GATT.

Chakravarthi Rhagavan speaks of the WTO entering "the developing world like a thief in the night".[1] The most dangerous and surreptitious aspect of this covert approach, from the point of view of

1

the developing countries, is that known as the 'single undertaking'. As with the negotiation of the Havana Charter and the ongoing trade negotiations for more than 40 years under the GATT, the developing nations were marginalised in the Uruguay Round negotiations. However, to the extent that they did take part, they did so in the belief that the resultant organisation would operate on the same agreement-by-agreement basis that GATT had done. It was only in late 1990 that developing countries became aware that, by joining the proposed international trading body, they would be contracting themselves to each and every one of its agreements.

The current selection of readings enters the fray in 1981, shortly after the launch of the daily, Geneva based, *South-North Development Monitor* (SUNS) from which a number of the earlier pieces reproduced here are drawn. Chakravarthi Raghavan, who single handedly produces the SUNS was one of the few southern anlaysts of the multilateral trading system at this time and hence his name appears frequently in the first section of this volume. By 1981, the GATT had been operating for 34 years and was comfortably settled into the habits that would mark its entire life span and be carried over into the functioning of the WTO.

Section 1 of this collection deals with the GATT period and demonstrates that, already by the beginning of the 1980s, many of the areas raised by later critics of the WTO system were manifesting themselves as problems for the developing countries. The WTO existed alongside the original GATT for some time in 1995. Chakravarthi Raghavan notes elsewhere[2] that,

> It was decided that the WTO and its GATT 1994 should legally be separate from GATT 1947, and not a continuous system…Yet, in practice WTO/GATT 1994 is being made to appear a continuing system - to enable the WTO to claim some of the legitimacy of the post-war institutions.

The two pieces extracted from SUNS of this period note firstly, the lack of transparency of the GATT system and, secondly, a shift from 'free trade' to 'managed trade'. In the first case, while insiders to GATT debate the significant issue of the power and/or fallibility of the market as a defining economic force, the writer notes that to anyone outside the

[1] Raghavan, C. (1999) *From GATT to the WTO: The Secret Story of the Uruguay Round through Fifteen Years of Daily Reports* (CD ROM), Penang: Third World Network.
[2] Raghavan, C. Ibid.

power structures of the WTO and the international financial institutions (including many GATT contracting party states) the GATT Emperor's clothes will not be revealed for judgement. In fact, the Emperor, as has been the case for over thirty years will not be coming out of the closet of the conference room at all. Secondly, the movement from 'free' to 'managed' trade is reflected in the introduction of 'flexible protection', the flexibility of which is mainly of advantage to the industrialised countries, while there is continuing inflexibility in allowing protective measures that might benefit the developing countries. Miles Kahler and John Odell touch on this theme again in a later piece.

Events to mark 40 years of the GATT in 1987 celebrate economic liberalism in general and, specifically, the continuing and widening liberalisation of international trade. A broader political hegemony embraces this and becomes apparent when Willy De Clerc of the European Economic Commission is adamant that the Soviet Union is not eligible to become a contracting party. The prevailing ideology, even before the introduction of the Dispute Settlement Mechanism under the WTO is enforceable by other means. Paul Volcker, Chair of the US Federal Reserve from 1979 to 1987, calls upon international financial institutions to provide needed financing for countries liberalising trade, "or conversely, by withdrawing finance" from those who do not. This tendency to control and manipulate can be traced through the GATT and WTO periods to the recent flashing of 'Bush's Billions' promised at the United Nations Financing for Development Conference in Monterrey, Mexico,

> We must tie greater aid to political and legal and economic reforms. And by insisting on reform, we do the work of compassion. The United States will lead by example. I have proposed a 50-percent increase in our core development assistance over the next three budget years. Eventually, this will mean a $5-billion annual increase over current levels.

Within the context described in Raghavan's piece, Miles Kahler and John Odell examine the notion of a developing country coalition in the Uruguay Round negotiations. Noting the developing world's history of non-involvement in previous trade rounds, they question whether such a coalition might be a means to increase developing country participation and, if so, what form or forms it might take. It is interesting to note that none of the issues they identify (textiles, agriculture, debt, international financing, commodities), even those that were taken up in the Uruguay Round and included in the WTO, has been resolved in a way that is satisfactory for the developing countries.

Section 2 covers the transition period and looks into the details of the Uruguay Round Agreements.

Chandrakant Patel, in this section, examines the notion of a 'single undertaking' which arose in the course of the Uruguay Round. He looks at the impetus for its introduction, primarily by the US, and the various interpretations that the term might be given, finding that the interpretation 'all results of all negotiations should be applied as a single package to all parties' is the one adopted in the Final Act of the Uruguay Round. Because of their weak bargaining positions and lack of negotiations capacity, and because the content of many of the agreements in the Uruguay Round 'package' were of little relevance to them, this was the interpretation least beneficial to the developing country members of the nascent WTO.

Extracts from two UNCTAD documents produced in 1994 provide an analysis of the Uruguay Round Agreements, noting in particular the dramatic increase in the number and scope of obligations of the developing countries and predicting exactly the sort of implementation problems that have dogged the developing countries in the WTO from its inception to the present. The piece by Magda Shahin looks specifically at the Dispute Settlement Understanding of the WTO questioning its efficacy for weaker partners in a dispute. Raghavan writes from the cusp of the transition, in the specific context of US relations with Japan. He demonstrates the failure of the principle of 'good faith'. In line with the Vienna Law of Treaties, the WTO ought to operate on the basis of "free consent, good faith and full implementation". The US had consented freely to the WTO Agreements. Its level of implementation was still to be tested when the Agreements came into force. But during the transition period, rather than 'good faith' which would have seen it already adopting the type of behaviour it had agreed to under the Uruguay Round, the US adopted a 'stag party' approach, seeking to have as much fun as possible before settling down to the strictures of the WTO system.

The piece by Bhagirath Lal Das in this section was actually written shortly after the collapse of the Seattle Ministerial Meeting in November 1999, i.e. well into the WTO regime, and thus suggests a lack of positive change in the way the GATT/WTO system has operated. The non-inclusive processes that were inherited from the

GATT system are seen as a direct cause of the formal and informal protests that took place around the Seattle meeting. Das outlines, on a practical level, how the negotiating processes in the WTO work and suggests the type of mechanism that could be established within the WTO to allow them to work better.

Section 3 explores the nexus of the WTO system and its developing country members questioning the extent to which the developing countries are ready for and capable of effective participation in the WTO.

The Southern and Eastern African Trade Information and Negotiations Initiative (SEATINI) was formed in 1998 to strengthen Africa in world trade, initially by equipping African trade negotiators with the skills and information they needed to work competently within the WTO. While Yash Tandon's piece, which arises directly from the first SEATINI workshop, examines the capacity of developing countries to use the system to any sort of advantage, Bahgirath Das turns to the WTO Agreements themselves and looks at how they are structured to disadvantage the developing world. As Das states,

> One of the main objectives of the proponents of the Uruguay Round was to obtain commitments and concessions from developing countries and it is no surprise that the final result is heavily weighted towards fulfilment of that objective.

In examining the Agreements one by one, Das uncovers their general tendency to perpetuate the trading strength and advantage of the industrialised world at the expense of the developmental, or simply survival, objectives of the weaker 'partners' to the Agreements. The Agreement on Agriculture, for example, binds developing countries to very low, or zero, levels of protection while ignoring the effect that this potentially has on their food security. Under the Services Agreement, there is a specific provision allowing cross-border movement of capital (a point of interest to richer countries seeking to invest and then repatriate funds) but no corollary provision on the movement of persons (an issue of importance to poorer countries with a large labour force and, often, problems of unemployment). These imbalances are not new. Pakistan Trade Minister, Mahbub Ul-Haq, in 1987 (page 31 this volume), supports the extension of GATT to new areas, including services but notes that there must be inbuilt assurances that developing countries will not be discriminated against in those areas where they have a comparative advantage.

A joint report of the UNCTAD and WTO secretariats, presented in mid 1998, confirms these tendencies, highlighting that improvements in market access were focused on areas of interest to developed countries while products of export interest to developing countries still faced significant tariff peaks and tariff escalation.

The piece by Vinod Rege in this section examines the imbalances of the Uruguay Round Agreements further in the context of two case studies conducted by the Commonwealth Secretariat around specific agreements. In summary, the studies of the Customs Valuation and Pre-Shipment Inspection Agreements find that negotiations are dominated by the two major players, the US and EU, who are well prepared in terms of lobbying in other forums beforehand but poorly prepared when it comes to understanding the needs and perspectives of those they are negotiating with. Rege looks at issues of knowledge examining the concepts of 'rational ignorance' in which actors proceed on the basis of incorrect premises, and 'the veil of uncertainty', under which actors act defensively for fear of the unknown consequences of more positive action.

A lack of appropriate knowledge is deeply imbedded in the development of the GATT and the WTO. The major powers could be said to be 'willfully' rather than just 'rationally' ignorant as they have little desire to see things from the perspective of weaker partners. Those in the developing world did not realise that what was being negotiated under the Uruguay Round was to be applied on a single undertaking basis (rational ignorance). In addition, developing country negotiators have constantly worked under a veil of uncertainty, caused by insufficient knowledge of the Agreements and their possible implications that has limited them to attempting to 'contain the damage' rather than asserting a positive agenda in the interest of their countries. Though there are forces both inside and outside developing countries obstructing the flow of knowledge, the challenge is thrown back to developing countries to assert their needs on the basis of sound information and broad national consultation.

It would be encouraging to suggest a light at the end of the tunnel. As yet, it is a dim one but could be made to burn brighter by the application of clear strategies towards improving the position of the developing countries within the global trading system. Bhagirath Das's piece outlines the institutional innovations needed in developing countries to enable them to better cope with the WTO. Where his earlier piece suggests structures within the WTO system itself, here he suggests what could be done at a national level. His suggestions, in both cases, are thoughtful and detailed, providing, at the very least, ample food for thought and debate.

Finally, the summary report of the first SEATINI Workshop, a synthesis of five days' debate among African trade negotiators, Geneva based officials, NGO representatives and trade experts, is reproduced here for the clear direction it suggested at the conclusion of these discussions in 1998.

Section 1
THE RULES OF THE GAME: The GATT Period

GATT AND THE EMPEROR'S CLOTHES
Chakravarthi Raghavan

"GATT and the Emperor's Clothes" was originally published by Inter Press Service (IPS) on 6 November 1982. It gives a concise history to the General Agreement on Tariffs and Trade (GATT) of 1947. Written some years before 'transparency' became a major demand made of governments and organisations, Raghavan's piece examines the emergence of non-transparency in the GATT. What is presented to the public is the notion that the growth and prosperity that followed World War II was attributable to the GATT system and obedience to the laws of the market. What lies hidden is the contention of many in the third world by 1982 that the GATT, in fact, responded to new production structures and trade flows which were the source of economic growth.

GATT's hour of truth will be in October and November, when decisions have to be made and a mere formulation of words will not do, the Director General of the General Agreement on Tariffs and Trade, Mr Arthur Dunkel said in August 1982 in an interview.

October has come and gone and, in the last week of November, the ministers will be around in Geneva.

In the fable, the Emperor and his citizens were able to see the truth when a child, innocent and unafraid, saw no fine gold clothes on the Emperor and shouted that the Emperor was naked. But no such child, nor any outsider, will be present when the ministers and their entourages meet in Geneva's International Conference Centre. With all the fanfare of media buildup and publicity that has been going on for months, as now scheduled, the press will not be allowed in either.

It was in 1946 that the United Nations General Assembly laid down the basic policy of the organisation to public information and access to it. With refinements over time this is still the basic guideline for the UN system.

But GATT being a 'contract' and an 'agreement' has always been closed to the public and the press, and no press freedom committee anywhere has protested though they raise vociferous campaigns when UNESCO holds a small consultation in private.

At GATT, the press has to depend on briefings by the official spokesperson or talk to delegates. It has no access officially, even to the basic documents and reports before a meeting. With all the professional competence and desire to be helpful on the part of the spokespersons, they function within the limitations of the dominant structures of GATT. If third world views are less well known than those of the industrialised world, and within it those of the USA and the EEC, it is also due to the transnational information system and the fact that there is less than a handful of press reporting for third world media from Geneva.

Third world countries are increasingly concerned about this and are trying to get the Ministerial meeting, at least, thrown open to the press, though they know even this will have only limited effect on the reportage. The US and EEC views will still be covered globally, while those of other individual countries might be lucky to be reported back at home.

In the over a score of international and intergovernmental organisations spawned in the postwar world, with the founding of the United Nations in the name of the peoples of the world, GATT is a peculiar animal.

It began as the General Agreement on Tariffs and Trade and was intended to be only a temporary arrangement for multilateral trade until the more permanent framework envisaged in the Havana Charter, the International Trade Organisation, came into being and took over.

But, the US Senate would have none of it. Deep protectionist fears over low cost production from Europe prevailed and the ITO was aborted.

Even then, for a long time, GATT continued its temporary existence. It had no secretariat of its own. The Agreement was administered by the Interim Commission for an International Trade Organisation (ICITO), with the main function of registering the commitments entered into under the General Agreement. The term 'secretariat' for GATT, when it came into vogue, was spelt only with a small 's' and its executive was called the 'executive secretary', becoming the Director General only in 1963.

GATT, and the diplomats accredited to it, in fact, pride themselves on being a 'contract' and 'agreement' rather than an 'organisation' like the other specialised agencies (WHO, FAO etc.) or organs of the General Assembly, like UNCTAD and UNIDO.

It was John Collins Bossidy who said, in 1910,

And this is good old Boston
the home of the bean and the cod
where the Lowells talk to the Cabots
and the Cabots talk only to God.

Among the international organisations, this about sums up the relationship of the plebian and universal UN and its agencies on the one hand to the, less universal but more powerful, IMF-IBRD-GATT system on the other. The god, supplanting those of all religions (Hinduism, Judaism, Christianity, Islam et al) is 'the market'. Bossidy never told us whether God talked to Cabots; nor do we know whether the market talks to this trio but they are the prophets of this God and even the ungodly Marxists are beginning to listen to them.

Unintentionally, but symbolically nevertheless, this special relationship is reflected in the tentative schedule recommended by the preparatory committee for the three day Ministerial meeting. On its opening day, 24 November, the morning session will hear some ministers and the chief executives of the IMF and the World Bank. On the next day will come the turn of the United Nations (perhaps through the Director General for International Economic Cooperation, the second highest ranking person in the entire UN system) and, last, the Secretary General of the United Nations Conference on Trade and Development.

An unconventional new wisdom, one which accepts market theories but refuses to deify the market, is that the roots of growth and prosperity lay elsewhere and GATT merely accommodated itself to the new production structures and trade flows. This implies that, unless it again accommodates itself to the new realities - new production structures, and economic and trade weights in the world of the socialists and third world, it would collapse. This might be too much for the GATT and the ministers to it to accept, for it puts most of them out of business.

The traditional wisdom of GATT and the prophets of the market is that postwar growth and prosperity was due to the GATT system and obedience to the laws of the market. The non-traditional, yet market oriented philosophy (as represented by UNCTAD), is that postwar growth and prosperity was essentially due to the fact that Europe and Japan were able to rebuild through exceptions and departures from GATT principles.

If GATT wisdom is correct, ministers must go back to pristine GATT, free trade principles and roll back both blatant and hidden protectionist measures. If non-traditional wisdom is right, either one must go back to first principles, providing special treatment favoring the third world, or one must accept the realities of 'managed trade' and bring it under the discipline of agreed rules and multilateral surveillance.

What will the ministers do? Will they see the truth or will it elude them?

FROM FREE TRADE TO MANAGED TRADE
Chakravarthi Raghavan

"From Free Trade to Managed Trade" was first published by IPS on 2 October 1981. In the period between the Tokyo Round of trade negotiations (1973-79) and the Uruguay Round there was a discernible movement by the industrialised countries towards 'managing' the flow of imports through a range of protectionist mechanisms. Ostensibly, such mechanisms are also available for developing countries to use but, in a system based on bargaining, these countries have little to offer in order to extract major concessions. Thus, the trend towards managed trade is controlled by those who already have the most power and consequently further weakens the developing countries. At the end of this piece, Raghavan cites the opinion of UNCTAD advisor R. G. Figueredo that it is time for "an improved, more comprehensive, more realistic, and universal system". He may well have had in mind something along the lines of the World Trade Organisation. The papers in Sections 2 and 3 of this volume discuss how effective, or otherwise, such a system has been in truly liberalising trade to the benefit of all players.

Unconditional most favoured nation (MFN) treatment has now ceased to be the guiding principle of international trade relations and has given place to 'managed' trade, with flexible mechanisms benefiting limited groups of countries and with less favourable treatment for the third world, according to UNCTAD.

This assessment of the international trade regime in GATT, in the

---

[3] UNCTAD Report TD/B/1101, 2 July 1986.

period following the Tokyo Round of multilateral trade negotiations was given to UNCTAD's Trade and Development board by the UNCTAD Director of Manufactures Division, Mr R.G. Figueredo.

Assessing the overall results and, as he put it, looking beyond the sum of its parts (tariff reductions, non-tariff agreements, understandings etc), Figueredo said as a result of the multilateral trade negotiations, "international trade relations are being conducted within the framework of a system that presents different characteristics from that which existed in 1973 when the Tokyo Declaration was drawn up".

There was now a decline in the importance of fixed measures of protection, especially customs duties, whose incidence however tended to be greater on imports from third world countries.

There was now greater reliance on mechanisms of 'flexible protection', for application of measures in specific conditions. Such protective measures, based upon interpretations of various terms and criteria have been influenced by a tendency towards 'managed' trade.

While tariffs and residual quantitative restrictions, and discriminatory non-tariff measures have been gradually liberalised, these have not been evenly distributed. The average tariffs facing third world exports was now frequently two to three times those that applied to imports from industrialised countries. Residual quantitative restrictions are concentrated on products where the third world countries are major suppliers.

This outcome, in Figueredo's view, has been due to two factors. Firstly, the third world has been unable to exercise the bargaining power necessary to achieve tariff concessions on products where it is the principal or substantial supplier. Secondly, the OECD countries have been unwilling to make or seek tariff reductions in products where they have lost, or are rapidly losing, their comparative advantage in international trade.

This is also because the negotiating processes under GATT are based on concepts of reciprocity and mutuality of advantages, where the third world has little to offer in order to extract major concessions.

With their reliance now on 'flexible protective measures', the industrialised countries during the Tokyo Round paid much attention to 'contingent' protection subsidies and countervailing measures, anti-dumping code, and the safeguards system (where they sought selective safeguard rights). Since there was no agreement on the last, important protective measures, such as voluntary export restraints, are now left outside the GATT legal framework. Other flexible protective measures, like the 'trigger price' mechanism for steel, or the Multi-Fibre Agreeement (MFA), that institutionalised the 'contingent' protection in textiles and clothing, have been left out of the negotiations.

Such flexible measures do not represent mutual balance of advantages. Interpretations of various terms for such measures 'serious injury', 'injury', 'material injury', 'serious damage', 'market disruption or threat or real risk thereof', 'subsidised and dumped exports at prices substantially lower than those prevailing in the importing country', 'disruption', 'unfair competition' etc. - all relate to situations in the importing country and the character of the imports themselves.

Combinations of these concepts are now used to provide the legal and political justification for protectionist steps, over and above the bound tariffs.

While some of these terms would over a period of time become defined by case law under the GATT dispute settlement procedures, the terms defined in particular instances in disputes involving a limited number of countries would become inappropriate for general and universal application, Figueredo commented.

Under the multilateral trade negotiations, the concern for flexibility in protectionist measures has been as, if not more, important than the drive for liberalised trade.

Under the 'managed trade' concept, instead of tariff barriers, the importing country decides the quantities and prices of imported products to be sold in its domestic markets. This concept has arisen mainly because the current system has been unable to provide a legal mechanism to deal adequately with shifts in comparative advantage from one country or group of countries to others. The already existing discriminations, like quantitative restrictions against 'low cost' suppliers or those favouring members of customs unions or free trade areas who accept an equivalent level of rights and obligations, had been worsened on the basis of whether a country had or had not accepted new obligations on a reciprocal basis under the negotiations.

Instead of the GATT contract obligation of more favourable treatment to developing countries, there was now less favourable treatment to them.

The reason why the unconditional MFN clause, so vociferously defended over so many years, was being given up is because of the implicit recognition by the major economic powers that the original GATT system could not be effectively applied in a universal context.

While it could be argued that the system was adapting itself to changing circumstances, it was questionable as to how long a system could be maintained that paid lipservice to general principles and rules but whose main role now was of providing a judicial framework for bestowing legality on measures conflicting with such rules and principles.

The UNCTAD Director argued that it was time to conceive a new system, of a more universal, comprehensive and coherent nature rather than the present ad hoc one. In his view, it was time to begin considering what new or revised, principles and policies would be necessary to resolve the contradictions in the international trading system and provide the basis for an improved, more comprehensive, more realistic, and universal system.

NOTES ON DEVELOPMENTS IN THE INTERNATIONAL TRADING SYSTEM FOR THE REVIEW UNDER CONFERENCE RESOLUTION 159(VI), PARAGRAPH 14, AND BOARD DECISION 320(XXXI) (extract)
UNCTAD Secretariat

This piece is extracted from a report to the 33rd Session of the Trade and Development Board held in Geneva in September 1986.[3] Conference Resolution 159 (VI), with which it deals, is concerned with International Trade in Goods and Services: Protectionism, Structural Adjustment and the International Trading System. The report begins to highlight the built in inequities already emerging under the GATT and the tendency for powerful players to ignore or circumvent those rules that do not work in their favour. In such a setting, the report finds, it has not been possible for third world countries to exploit trade as a tool for development. The report concludes with some recommendations for the improvement of the system. The remainder of this volume and others in the series will examine to what extent these were, or were not, taken up.

Note: the footnote references are in line with those in the rest of this volume and do not reflect the footnote numbering in the original document.

Chapter 1

THE CONTINUED EROSION OF THE MULTILATERAL TRADING SYSTEM

A. *Diagnosis*

1. The failure or erosion of the multilateral system, which has been manifested by a variety of symptoms, has been studied by the international community in UNCTAD, GATT and elsewhere.[4] These studies have identified, as the main symptoms of the erosion of the system

    (a) A neglect of the unconditional most-favoured-nation clause, the fundamental principle of GATT, particularly through the application of discriminatory trade measures applied, in the main, against developing countries and usually in the form of so-called voluntary export restraints, or the "conditional" application of codes on non-tariff measures;

    (b) An increased resort to managed trade mechanisms, which involve a control of the qualities, price and often the sources of imports;

    (c) The use of arrangements in favour of the developing countries (notably GSP) to obtain negotiating leverage with those countries;

    (d) The inadequacies of conciliation and dispute-settlement procedures;

    (e) The use of trade measures for non-economic objectives;

    (f) A failure to respect multilateral obligations in national legal systems. An opposite tendency now appears evident, i.e. that of attempting to modify multilateral commitments so as to legitimize practices providing for in domestic trade law;

    (g) An increase in recourse to bilateral rather than multilateral arrangements;

    (h) The continued maintenance of measures inconsistent with

---

[4] The first analysis in this respect was conducted in the Trade and Development Board. See report of 23rd session of the Trade and Development Board as well as TD/B/914,848,1005 and TD/274, confirmed later in several articles in Cline (ed.) and Trade Policy in the 1980's, Washington, Institute for International Economics, 1983, especially that by H.B. Malmgren. Also the independent study recently published by GATT: *Trade Policies for a Better Future: Recommendations for Action,* GATT Geneva 1985.

GATT and attempts to secure concessions in return for the removal of such measures;

(i) There has been a notable expansion of countertrade, not only between developing countries but also between developing countries and developed market economy countries. The existence of countertrade testifies to the need felt by countries for action outside the market price-directed systems.

2. These studies have expressed concern that trade relations are increasingly based on power relationships rather than respect for contractual commitments.

Despite efforts to improve and refine dispute settlement mechanisms, during and after the Tokyo Round, the process of settling disputes, particularly that of obtaining the consequent corrective policy actions on the part of countries found to be in conflict with their multilateral obligations, is proving to be an increasingly frustrating process. To only a very limited extent can this be attributed to inadequacies in the procedures for dispute settlement.[5] The fact that the ultimate resources for a party "winning" a case is to withdraw compensatory concessions is obviously a deterrent to weaker partners seeking enforcement of their rights; the larger countries do not easily tolerate retaliation against themselves. Disputes are arising more frequently among the major industrial powers largely provoked by the different perceptions of the mutual balance of advantages mentioned above, particularly with respect to subsidies and the participation in customs unions and other preferential arrangements.[6] In many cases these conflicts between developed countries are settled outside of GATT. Many developing countries are hesitant to use this mechanism, considering that the impact of whatever action they could take might not be enough as to influence the behaviour of major industrial of major industrial countries, in addition to recognizing the economic costs inherent in such trade restrictive action.

3. As has been noted in earlier documentation, these tendencies can

---

[5] As has been pointed out by the GATT Director-General, too long delays in getting the disputants to accept and implement the findings of the panels' reports "is an indication of lack of political will to make the system work", *International Trade Reporter*, 12 February 1986.

[6] Disputes among developed countries have centred on the agricultural sector, largely between the EEC and the USA, including with respect to subsidies, tariff preferences and EC enlargement, as well as on various aspects of the Japanese import regime and specific protective devices maintained by the United States.

be attributed, to a significant degree, to the fact that the GATT system was based on a series of policy assumptions. At the time of the Bretton Woods agreement and the Havana Charter there was a policy consensus at a high political level among the major trading countries as to their economic policy objectives. For the trade relations area, these were set out in the Havana Charter. Chapter IV of that Charter, which became the GATT, dealt essentially only with mechanisms and procedures. Given the assumption of a market system, the key trade policy mechanism was to be the customs duty. Rules governing other trade measures (i.e. non-tariff measures and "safeguards") were incorporated in order to preserve the integrity of the tariff concessions.[7]

4.   Developing countries are finding it difficult to avoid the perceptions that industrialized countries are not prepared to accept a steady increase in imports, even from a very limited number of developing countries,[8] in sectors where such imports compete in any significant way with their domestic production.

The major importing countries react with a variety of trade obstructing measures, some technically legal under GATT, including measures under special waivers, or falling within the "grey area" outside of multilateral disciplines. The net effect is to threaten to confine developing countries to a limited, "acceptable", and often insignificant, share of world markets in such product sectors as they may be able to develop a competitive edge. This has underlined the real limits to export-oriented policies as a generally applicable approach to economic development, and has provided Governments with an incentive to examine alternative models of growth, particularly those aimed at "regional economic security".[9]

5.   Any attempt to strengthen and improve the trading system must address the fundamental issues that have led to the erosion of the system, both those which are exogeneous to the trading system *per se*, examined in chapter II and those inherent to the trading systems, which are discussed in the following paragraphs...

---

[7] Evoked by J. Jackson "Developing Country Relationship to GATT in the Post-MNT Era", UNCTAD/MTN/205, Geneva, 1981, "GATT Machinery and the Tokyo Round Agreements" in his article in Trade Policy in the 1980s, *op.cit.*,pp.159-187.

[8] Usually defined as between 7-10 fast growing exporters among developing countries.

[9] See Decision 174 "Regional Economic Security" of the Latin American Council and the Quito Declaration and Plan of Action adopted by the Latin American Economic Conference, January 1984.

C. The integrity of the unconditional most-favoured-nation clause

7.   The unconditional MFN clause of Article I of the General Agreement was to be the basis of the multilateral trading system. While many formal exceptions have been made under the GATT procedure (e.g. customs unions, free trade areas under Article XXIV, GSP) which have modified the applicability of the clause, these have not called into question the status of the unconditional MFN clause as the "cornerstone" of the system. However, unilateral deviations from unconditional MFN threaten to completely undermine the working of the MFN clause...

8.   The trend towards narrowly conceived bilateral reciprocity and consequent discrimination against third countries was part and parcel of the collapse of the world trading system in the 1930s. The architects of the post-war multilateral system were well aware of this when they accepted the unconditional most-favoured-nation clause as the basis for the commercial policy chapter of the Havana Charter (i.e. the GATT).

D. The enforcement of rights and obligations

9.   The GATT system relies on retaliation as the ultimate recourse for enforcement of rights. This handicaps the weaker trading partners because retaliation may not always be possible for them, or may have little economic effect on major trading countries. Of course, the demonstration effect can have political impact. It has been proposed that the system should be strengthened through resort to joint action by all signatories when the rights of one signatory is in jeopardy.[10] However, only a clearer political and legal commitment by the major trading countries to abide by the rules can generate confidence in the system.

10.   The issues of security of access and of enforcement of rights and obligations are obviously two aspects of the same problem. Underlying

---

[10] This has been an outstanding proposal by developing countries, however, the 1996 Decision on Procedures under Article XXII (GATT, BISD/14S) and the 1979 Understanding regarding Notification, Consultation, Dispute Settlement and Surveillance (BISD/26S, p.18) only refer to the possibility of the Contracting Parties taking "further action" which might be "appropriate to the circumstances" (BISD/16S, p.124).

both is a widely held perception that the major trading countries, if pressed, will tend to ignore their multilateral obligations, and therefore that it is more prudent to "make a deal" or, euphemistically, "adopt a pragmatic approach", even though this implies sacrificing fundamental rights to market access and to non-discriminatory treatment. The erosion of the trading system is largely the result of the accumulated effect of such "pragmatic" solutions...

E.   *Multilateral Reciprocity*

12.   Developing countries' ability to obtain concessions in multilateral trade negotiations has been hindered by the fact that they are usually not the principle suppliers of products of vital interest to them, and that they are unable to offer meaningful reciprocity. The result has been to increase imbalances or the benefits under GATT, most apparent in the relatively higher tariff rates that are generally applied in sectors predominantly of interest to developing countries...

F.   *The future of the tariff-based system*

14.   The operation of the unconditional MFN clause and the general reciprocity criterion were facilitated by another guiding principle of the system: that the trade flows should be determined by prices determined in markets, and that, therefore, the tariff was the only acceptable means of protection (except in clearly defined exceptional circumstances).

15.   As has been stated above, the reliance on flexible or "contingent" measures, rather than fixed levels of protection, has greatly increased...

G.   *Unfair trade*

17.   ...The concept of "unfair practices" is being extended in domestic trade legislation to cover a wider range of practices than those specifically identified in GATT. Protectionist and discriminatory actions are being portrayed as a simply legitimate defence against unfair practices, and there is increased scope for harassment as a protectionist tactic.

H.   *Subsidies*

18.   With respect to the disciplining of subsidies, the trading system has become in the extreme. Developing countries' scope for providing export incentives on manufactured goods is being continually reduced

through the ever more stringent application of countervailing duties, but their export opportunities for agricultural products are being eroded by subsidies by the major industrial powers, which are, of course, often major agricultural producers as well...

J. *Commodity prices*

21. An international trading system which does not provide for multilateral commitments with respect to international commodity prices has little relevance to those many countries which depend upon the export of primary commodities. This logic lay behind the inclusion of commitments with respect to raw materials and to commodity arrangements in the Havana Charter. Commodity price fluctuations make it impossible for such countries to maintain a consistent trade policy regime; it is difficult for such countries to accept disciplines with respect to their import regime because their ability to import is a function of their export earnings from commodities which tend to be erratic, and in the long term, to decline.

L. *Transnational corporations (TNCs)*

23.   ...Earlier rounds of trade negotiations were often presented as designed to permit corporations to invest in exportoriented production in their home country so as not to "transfer" jobs abroad, by reducing the necessity of foreign investment to serve protected markets abroad. On the other hand, the success of these rounds provoked the concern that foreign investments might largely be intended to produce for export to the home market, taking account of lower labour costs. In the main home countries of TNCs, the national TNCs are now seen as "national champions" in the development of new technologies in product innovation and in the penetration of exports markets for goods and services.[11] Governments wishing to promote the competitiveness of "their" TNCs are less likely to place barriers in the way of investment and production abroad where this contributes to this competitiveness.

24.   Developing countries, which, unlike developed market-economy countries, tend to be almost exclusively "host" countries, have applied a

---

[11] See Stein Rossen in Notes on Rules and Mechanisms Governing International Economic Relations (1983, TD/274), Bergen, Norway, Chr. Michelsen Institute.

variety of measures to ensure that the practices of TNCs conform to their development strategies...

25. Governments, particularly those of developing countries, have recognized the importance of TNCs in international trade, and the inadequacy of multilateral trade disciplines which ignore their existence. They appear reluctant to accept any multilateral rules or concessions that might reduce the scope of action for maintaining effective control over TNCs, unless an effective multilateral framework can be established for this purpose...

M.   *Response of the international trading community*

26.   An insecure trading environment undermines the willingness to make investment in developing countries required to permit significant restructuring, and to maintain competitiveness in world markets...

31.   Although they may not have lived up to expectations, both the GATT Ministerial Session and UNCTAD VI produced certain positive results. The GATT Ministerial Work Programme has identified goals in precise areas. UNCTAD Conference resolution 159(VI) contains a series of specific commitments and recognition of the need for action on various issues. Paragraphs 14, in particular, embodies a universal commitment to a strengthened and improved trading system and outlines the characteristics of such a system. On the surface, therefore, it would seem that negotiations will not only be doomed to failure, but could also exacerbate the decline rather than improve the system if they avoid taking into account not only the fundamental trade policy issues at stake but also the underlying economic and political factors which have led to the erosion of the international trading system.

32.   It should be noted that it was intended in the Havana Charter that the rules and disciplines of the trading system would cover a much wider range of measures than the tariff bindings and related disciplines contained in the General Agreement on Tariffs and Trade. Much of the erosion of the GATT system can be attributed to the fact that GATT was (and is) only a part of the agreed Havana proposals...

Chapter 3

INITIATIVES TO STRENGTHEN AND IMPROVE THE TRADING SYSTEM

G. *Concluding remarks*

82.   The stresses on the international trading system are to a large part due to developments outside the trade policy domain. However, the strengthening and improvement of the system cannot be left until solutions are reached with respect to these exogenous factors. On the contrary, by definition, a stronger and improved system should be capable of providing the framework for trade relations in a rapidly changing trading world, and could strengthen the resolve of the international trading community in dealing with monetary issues and in achieving a greater degree of harmony in their macroeconomic policies.

83.   The main purpose of this document, and the contribution it has attempted to make in addition to the previous UNCTAD documents on the trading system, is to draw the attention of the trading community to the radical changes in the structure and determinants of international trade, and the fundamental principles of the international trading system which have been placed in question. If the international trading community does not address these factors in its efforts to strengthen and improve the trading system, whether in the context of multilateral trade negotiations or otherwise, these efforts will be doomed to failure and will inevitably result in an exacerbation of the current tendencies in international trade relations, with the consequent unfavourable effects on world development and on international relations in general.

84.   There are four elements which could form part of the international consensus mentioned above, (a) the new system should not penalize any country or group of countries simply due to the product composition of exports (this would call for concerted action in the areas of agriculture, textiles and basic commodities), (b) the system should not deny countries the possibility of taking the policy measures necessary to improve their situation, (i.e. in the areas of services and technology), (c) it should not penalize countries because of their economic systems, and (d) it should protect countries against predatory trade practices designed to disrupt world trade or pass on the cost of adjustment to trading partners.

85.   Efforts to negotiate improvements in the trading system should be taken in light of a recognition of the historical background of the system. The present multilateral system, centred on the General Agreement on Tariffs and Trade, is based on the principles that trade protection will be afforded through customs tariffs only, that all trade concessions will be extended on an unconditional most-favoured-nation basis, and that such concessions will be negotiated on the basis of multilateral reciprocity with developing countries receiving differential and more favourable treatment in this respect. It is also designed to deal with international flows of products and not of the factors of production.

86.   Unfortunately, the sum of the variety of proposals currently being advanced would suggest a movement toward a diametrically opposed system. There would appear to be danger that attempts may be made to bargain a return to greater security of access to markets for the establishment of a system based on conditionality and "managed" trade. However, security of access to markets and unconditional most favoured nation treatment remain the main supports of a dynamic trading system.

87.   The importance of universality was also recognized at Belgrade, and should be a major goal of trade negotiators. All countries should derive benefit from the system, regardless of their economic system or their product specialization.

88.   The most propitious manner for the Trade and Development Board to carry out its mandate under Conference resolution 159(VI) and Board decision 320(XXXI) could be to undertake detailed and in-depth studies of the forces which are radically affecting international trade and their manifestation in international trade relations. Only if the international community shares a common recognition of these factors can that consensus be reached which is a prerequisite for any meaningful strengthening and improvement of the trading system.

89.   It should be noted that, if multilateral trade negotiations are entered into, and particularly if their stated purpose is to strengthen and improve the international trading system, they cannot be allowed to fail. The main factor which could lead to the failure of the current international initiatives toward this objective is the absence of an underlying consensus. Negotiations are being initiated in a general atmosphere of disrespect for existing rules and principles of the system.

In such a situation it is the view of the UNCTAD secretariat that the most appropriate contribution that UNCTAD could make is to stimulate the consensus building process, through in-depth multilateral examination of the key elements involved.

36TH SESSION OF THE UNCTAD TRADE AND DEVELOPMENT BOARD, 1990 (extract)
UNCTAD Secretariat

This piece is extracted from the proceedings of the 36th Session of the Trade and Development Board of UNCTAD held in 1990.[12] It is a statement on behalf of the Group of 77 developing countries (G77) presented by Ambassador Azikiwe of Nigeria. In it, the Ambassador speaks of the increasing marginalisation of developing countries and their consequent inability to take advantage of development opportunities. While noting the openings offered by the Uruguay Round of trade negotiations (which eventually resulted in the launch of the WTO in 1994), the speaker expresses concern that the imbalances of the GATT may be further entrenched, rather than removed, by the negotiations.

Part II
SUMMARY OF PROCEEDINGS

Chapter 1
GENERAL STATEMENTS

19.   The spokesman for the Group of 77 (Nigeria) observed that, in the past decade, the role of developing countries in the world economy had become increasingly marginalized and their participation in international trade and finance had substantially decreased.

20.   The 1980s had been truly a lost decade for development and the Final Act of UNCTAD VII remained to a great extent a declaration of intent. Reviewing the background to the session, he said that the changes taking place in Eastern Europe and the new emerging regional economic integration groupings in the developed market economies were a turning point in international economic co-operation.

---

[12] UNCTAD Report TD/B/1257 (Vol II).

21.   The world of international trade was marked by changes in the trade of manufacturers, particularly in high technology products, which had been unpredictable in the last decades. New areas of trade in the services sector had opened up. Certain aspects of the current economic situation, particularly the widening economic and technological gap and the growing tendency towards the formation of trading blocs were a source of concern. The process of globalisation required a trade system that facilitated the exchange of goods and services, so that all the current trends towards regionalism should be channeled in such a way as to strengthen such exchanges. Trading blocs should contribute to the trade and development of the developing counties.

22.   He expressed the Group of 77's understanding for the countries of Eastern Europe as they moved towards greater integration into the world economy. It was his Group's sincere hope that this process should open new opportunities for the exports of developing countries and of the world economy as a whole. However, the developing countries, while welcoming the reawakening of international co-operation demonstrated in the solidarity shown by developed countries to the countries of Eastern Europe, were concerned that this process could lead to the further marginalisation of developing countries.

23.   The Uruguay Round had been widely acknowledged as the most complex and ambitious attempt to restructure the multilateral trading system, based on the GATT. The developing countries were convinced that it represented an opportunity to secure a fair and equitable and a more open, truly multilateral trading system, as a means of promoting the economic growth of all participants and the development of less developed participants. They has sought and obtained a political commitment for a balanced outcome of the results and for an operational reflection of their development needs and concerns in these results.

24.   Developing countries had reiterated their intention to continue to participate constructively in the Uruguay Round. They had, however, noted with deep concern the current lack of balance in the negotiations. In particular, attention had repeatedly been drawn to the evident imbalances in (i) the market access groups, especially tropical products and natural resource-based products; (ii) the apparent lack of political will to fully integrate textiles into GATT; (iii) the proposals to introduce selective safeguards as a permanent feature of the system; (iv) the

attempt to enlarge the scope of anti-dumping and countervailing duty rules and the employment of such measures as selective safeguard action; (v) the approach towards agriculture, which had a special sensitivity for developing countries, and (vi) the proposals and initiatives advanced in various negotiating groups aimed at depriving developing countries of their rights under GATT and at imposing obligations in disregard of their special needs and conditions. Unless corrective action was taken immediately a balanced outcome would be rendered that much more difficult and the prospects of the Uruguay Round being successfully and meaningfully concluded would be seriously jeopardized.

25.   Even whilst an intensification of the imbalance and asymmetry was being increasingly recognized, the Group of 77 had received indications that it was the intention of some industrialized countries to broaden the activities of the GATT under the umbrella of an International Trade Organisation (ITO). The motivation for this proposal appeared to stem from the perceived difficulties in implementing the results of the negotiations on TRIPs, TRIMs and services and dictated by a desire to consolidate the gains in favour of the owners of intellectual property, owners of capital and providers of services desirous of both exporting capital and know-how. The Punta del Este declaration clearly stipulated that Ministers, at their final meeting, would take a decision on the international implementation of the outcome of the Uruguay Round results. That decision should not be prejudged.

26.   The new initiative was clearly an effort to invoke the concept of the Havana Charter in form but not in substance. The Havana Charter contained several provisions now pursued by UNCTAD which were conspicuously absent in the new initiative. Several aspects of the restrictive features pursued by corporate entities had been ruled out of court by the industrialised countries which were the demanders in the negotiations on TRIPs and TRIMs where efforts were being made to create further rights for intellectual property owners and for owners of capital i.e. the investors. The entire thrust of the deliberations in these negotiating groups was to circumscribe the capacity of Governments to impose countervailing disciplines and obligations to fulfil the developmental requirements of their societies.

27.   Members of the Group of 77 would carefully consider a proposal to establish an international trade organization provided it was in line with the arrangements envisaged in resolution 1995 (XIX) and subsequent Conference resolutions. Such an organization should be meaningful, comprehensive and responsive to the developmental aspirations of developing countries, and will require careful and detailed preparation under the bodies of the United Nations which had both the comprehensive mandate and the universal membership experience and expertise to deal with such initiatives.

AT FORTY, GATT STILL A RICH MAN'S CLUB.
Chakravarthi Raghavan

"At Forty, GATT Still a Rich Man's Club" was originally published by IFDA, Geneva on 30 November 1987. Raghavan explores the nature of the GATT after 40 years of operation through a summary of the 'dialogue' on the day of the 'celebrations'. The interchange shows the developing countries denied any but the smallest voice. They are largely not invited and, the writer comments, would not be in a position to attend anyway. When their few representatives are given a rare chance to speak, their remarks are brushed aside, rather than followed up. Raghavan concludes that, after 40 years of the GATT, the developing world has little to celebrate.

The General Agreement on Tariffs and Trade (GATT) celebrated its 40th Anniversary Monday, with daylong events that perhaps showed, more than anything else, that GATT is still a rich man's club.

The day's events included reminiscences by three personalities associated with the founding of GATT, a keynote address by the former US Federal Reserve chairperson, Paul Volcker, and an afternoon of so called 'round table debate' involving Ministers, three chosen journalists and Prof. John Jackson, a US law professor and authority on GATT law.

Of the nineteen odd Ministers or people of equivalent rank participating, there were none from Africa and only two each from Asia and Latin America.

According to reports current among third world delegations, the entire format, including choice of journalists to put questions, had been made by the Secretariat in close consultation with the US delegation here.

GATT itself had issued no invitations to Ministers to attend, as is customary in other organisations. Even if they had, it was doubtful that any African countries could have afforded the luxury of coming here to 'celebrate' GATT, when it refuses to address their major problems commodity trade and debt.

"We will have a critical celebration" of the 40th Anniversary, GATT spokesperson David Woods had told news reporters last week in explaining the events planned.

> It is in no sense a meeting to signify self satisfaction or complacency, but an effort to present some kind of public face of GATT. So much of our work is complicated, and often unreportable, but we believe our work is not appreciated and we need the support of the business community and the general public.

In the day's events there was also considerable talk of the need for 'transparency' in government policies and, at one stage, the US Trade Representative, Clayton Yeutter, asked whether it would not be to the world's advantage if any restrictions any country imposed on import of 'services' were made transparent.

Yet GATT itself is the international institution that has the least transparency and functions most opaquely. No GATT meeting is held in public neither the press nor business or consumer NGOs are permitted to be present. GATT documents are all 'restricted' and released to the media only when they present a positive image of GATT. Those reporting on GATT must depend on their own lobbying or the briefing that GATT press officers give, but these mainly reflect the Secretariat views and those of the three major trading blocs.

GATT itself was founded as a temporary arrangement until the international trade organisation envisaged under the Havana Charter came into being. But the US Congress ultimately made clear it would say 'no' to the Havana Charter, and the proposed International Trade Organisation (ITO) never took off. GATT has remained, for 40 years now, a provisional treaty.

"It is only a treaty, and that too a provisional one, not at all a 'contract' that it is claimed to be", Prof. Jackson said Monday at the round table, and none of the Ministers or GATT officials present challenged him.

The ITO, and its provisional version in GATT, were part of the postwar economic system that owes its origins to Keynesian economic theories, modified by Dexter White to suit US interests. But neither Keynes nor White was a 'liberal' in the economic sense, meaning laissez faire economists. They and their governments believed in and saw the importance of the state's role and intervention to make the market function efficiently and honestly. There was little reference at the 40th Anniversary of GATT to any of this and everyone present talked of and assumed that the GATT order was intended to be, and should be, a 'liberal order'.

Paul Volcker perhaps went the farthest in this when he referred two or three times to the "liberal trade and investment order" that GATT should usher in to survive and be relevant. While Volcker's speech did not allow for questions, none of those in the afternoon debate challenged him either. Some among them, notably the Pakistan Minister Mahbub Ul-Haq and the Indian journalist Prem Shankar Jha, raised some inconvenient issues in terms of the neo-classical economics (in areas where the third world now has comparative advantage). But the phalanx of industrial country Ministers never answered them, or evaded any questions they were specifically asked.

There were many references to the problems of the monetary and financial system that were impinging on and damaging the world trading system and the need to address them. In introducing Volcker, the keynote speaker, GATT Director General, Arthur Dunkel, made many laudatory references to his achievements as Chair of the US Federal Reserve. Volcker, during his stewardship of the Federal Reserve, won plaudits from the central bankers of Europe, and perhaps even more the transnational banking community, for the huge profits they made as a result of the hiking of nominal and, more pertinently, 'real' interest rates in their loans to the third world and the fees they charged for renegotiating the loans. But if Volcker deserved all these plaudits, he surely also bore responsibility for the aftermath of these policies the debt crisis, the high interest rates that have made investment in production unprofitable and, an inevitable consequence, the October 29th crash.

But no one in the afternoon debate raised these questions.

And, in the last ten minutes, when a questioner from the floor, Jamaica's Anthony Hill, asked whether GATT and Trade Ministers would have been better off if there had been joint meetings of Trade and Finance Ministers, he got a reply from the New Zealand Minster, Michael Moore, to the effect that Trade Ministers and their Geneva representatives ought to meet more often. The moderator did not ask any other Minister to respond.

On they key issue of money and finance, and exchange rates, Volcker had little to say except his acknowledgement that the floating exchange rate system had belied all its promises of better equilibrium in national trade and current accounts, and said that, in practice, floating would result in "pretty steady" rates.

Volcker added,

> ...health and vitality of an international trading order will be importantly dependent over time upon the willingness of governments of large trading countries to reach some realistic collective judgements about the broadly appropriate level of exchange rates. Those judgements will, in turn, need to influence the design and implementation of domestic policies if they are to be meaningful and durable.

This wisdom has come two or three years too late, a third world delegate later commented.

Volcker spoke of the interlinkages between trade liberalisation efforts in GATT and the measures needed in the monetary and financial system but, even here, merely underscored the real politik in multilateralism. There was an impression in the US, he said, that the US had "the most open markets" of any major economic power, and there was a feeling of "unfairness" about this.

> Given those circumstances, I think we have to accept that American negotiators, in contrast to the past, will be unwilling and unable to offer concessions not visibly and fully matched by other countries.

He had little to say on the third world debt that he helped to aggravate through his interest rate policies, except for the view that efforts to restructure existing debt, finding new money, and restoring a sense of financial stability would continue to be of concern to Finance Ministers and central bankers, and that the IMF and the World Bank would have to play a leadership role they had been thrust into. But, he said, financial arrangements, however cleverly devised, could not substitute for more fundamental economic change and this could only be brought about through the agency of international trade in economic development.

He also referred to the many restrictions on third world exports the 'GATT sanctioned' Multi-Fibre Arrangement, the not so sanctioned 'grey area' measures of voluntary export restraints, the increasing reliance on 'safeguard' clauses and the non-application of GATT to agricultural trade.

While making these points to advocate the need to open up industrial country markets to third world exports, Volcker also called upon the newly industrialising and middle income countries to open up their markets and for GATT rules to provide criteria for 'graduating' these countries out of the ranks of 'developing countries' to whom the GATT principles of reciprocity would not apply.

Volcker also called upon international financial institutions to provide needed financing for countries liberalising trade, "or conversely, by withdrawing finance" from those who did not.

Of the three Latin American Ministers present, Brazil's Paul Tarso and Uruguay's Enrique Iglesias flagged the issue of Latin American indebtedness though neither of them, given the format of the meeting, had the opportunity even to outline the measures proposed by the eight Latin heads of states at Acapulco in Mexico over the weekend. Iglesias, however, stressed the vital link for third world countries between trade and development, and the need to find solutions to the third world debt problem through trade. The Latin debt servicing problems would be much less if only GATT rules were observed, Iglesias stated.

While the Ministers from the north suggested that there was no need for rewriting the GATT Charter, but only a need to make it relevant by extending it to new areas (like services, investment and intellectual property rights), Mahbub Ul-Haq challenged this and said structural changes would be needed, and among these would be greater enforceability and sanctions. If the industrial countries, he said at one point, had been forced to listen to IMF and World Bank advice and carry it out in relation to their budget or trade deficits, there would not be this current mess in the north (referring to the US borrowing in excess of its savings and budget and trade deficits). The industrial countries could ignore the IMF and the World Bank since they did not need credit from them, but they still needed GATT, and GATT could exercise some control over them, he suggested.

He also supported extension of GATT to new areas, including services, but said that any services framework should cover also movement of labour and capital, and should have built in assurances that, when third world countries acquired comparative advantage and ability, they would not be subject to discriminatory provisions as in the textiles and clothing sector through MFA or by VERS, and in footwear and other labour intensive manufactures. Haq also noted that different sectors of services were already being addressed by other international organisations so, before services could be brought under GATT, the GATT would have to earn third world confidence. He also called for an end to the MFA as part of the Uruguay round but got no response from his industrial country colleagues.

Haq also raised the issue of 'universality' vis à vis GATT, and said he could not see GATT being effective unless the Soviet Union and other Socialist Countries came in. But Willy De Clerc of the European Economic Commission rejected this by talking about the GATT's basis in 'free trade' and the need for homogeneity in a contract whose enforceability depended on acceptance by the parties involved. In effect, De Clerc made it clear that the Soviet Union could not be allowed to become a GATT Contracting Party.

The only socialist country Minister on the panel, Hungary's Foreign Trade Minister, Peter Veress, did not respond or challenge De Clerc on this.

Jackson and some others raised the issue of the enforceability of GATT, putting teeth into GATT, and how to make powerful countries carry out their obligations. But none of them raised the question that the only 'sanction' in GATT is the authorisation to the Contracting Party affected to 'retaliate', a power that the weak don't have, and even the strong like the EEC and Japan find difficult to use against the US. The GATT provisions in Article XXIII themselves envisage joint actions by Contracting Parties, i.e. collective sanctions but this has never been put into practice. However, none of the Ministers present, nor the journalists who were questioning, them raised this.

The issue of US sanctions against Nicaragua and the US invoking the GATT Article XXI (relating to national security exceptions) was raised by a journalist on the panel. The Swedish Minster to whom it was directed referred to the ruling of the panel in this case and need for enforcing it. Clearly, the Minister was unaware that the terms of the panel precluded it from going into the issue of Article XXI, and the journalist did not correct her on this. Yeutter said that no country, and no major country like the US, could be expected to submit its 'national security interests' to GATT judgement and there was no way the GATT could be changed in this regard.

In the final stages of this 'debate', the Nicaraguan delegate from the floor came back to the issue to correct the Swedish Minster and noted that the organs competent to go into this question (the UN

Security Council and General Assembly, and the International Court of Justice) had clearly ruled against the US and in favour of Nicaragua, and questioned whether GATT could survive if it did not tackle such matters. But Professor Jackson, to whom the question was addressed, in effect said that, since GATT could not force the US to obey and it was not in the interest of GATT to encourage evasions, it was best to solve the problem by expanding the scope of Article XXXV, which enables a Contracting Party to exclude another from benefits of its concession at the time of accession, to enable countries to withdraw concessions from other Contracting Parties even after accession.

Another major third world trade issue, liberalisation of trade in tropical products, on the GATT agenda since 1963 and a priority item in the Uruguay Round, figured only marginally in relation to discussions on agriculture. Both the US and the EEC, in the current Uruguay Round have been trying to merge the separate issue of tropical products into the agricultural negotiations. The moderator from the BBC brought up the issue at the end of the discussions on agriculture trade, which had been addressed as basically a temperate zone issue. The Indonesian Minister, Rachmat Saleh, who got a few minutes to deal with it, but only as part of the agricultural issue, underscored that the way the tropical products issue was dealt with would be the touchstone of the Uruguay Round for the third world, but did not outline the different issues involved.

DEVELOPING COUNTRIES AND THE GLOBAL TRADING SYSTEM
Miles Kahler and John Odell

"Developing Countries and the Global Trading System" was originally published in 1990, in one of a series of thematic studies from a Ford Foundation Project.[13] *The authors discuss the possibility of, and potential for, a developing country coalition in the Uruguay Round of trade negotiations, which, as discussed in the next section, led to the formation of the World Trade Organisation. They examine the way in which the marked differences between developing countries might*

---

[13] Whalley, J (ed) (1990) *Studies in International Trade Policy Vol I*, Ann Arbor: University of Michigan Press.

either inhibit or strengthen such a coalition. Among the issues mentioned are the Multi-Fibre Arrangement, which was in fact subsumed under the WTO as the Agreement on Textiles and Clothing, and agriculture which also became a WTO agreement. These two agreements are considered to be the Organisation's most development-friendly features. Also mentioned are the issues of commodities and debt which, in the event, developing countries were still struggling to have dealt with under the WTO at the end of the 20th century.

For much of the postwar era, the stance of developing countries towards international trade negotiations has encompassed two somewhat contradictory strategies. On the one hand, considerable energy has been expended in maintaining the unity of a developing country bloc that vocally expresses concern over the existing trading system and demands changes in it. On the other, they have adopted a relatively passive attitude toward the negotiation rounds themselves.[14] This strategy has long been criticised by northern sceptics and preparations for the Uruguay Round demonstrated discontent among some of the developing countries themselves. However, arguments for more active participation by developing countries in trade negotiations have seldom dealt specifically with the other strategies that could be pursued more successfully. Our examination of possible coalition strategies for the developing countries in the Uruguay Round and other international economic negotiations is motivated by an awareness of both the existing criticisms of the bloc strategy, previously endorsed by the G77, and the underlying logic of that strategy i.e. that, individually, the developing countries are not major powers in the international trading system. For those with less power, skilful strategies of coalition formation are a major implement for increasing success in such negotiations.

In examining coalition formation, a coalition is defined as two or more actors with shared interests that influence their bargaining behaviour toward other actors. This 'loose' definition of a coalition recognises that, in trade and other international economic negotiations, coalitions are often fleeting and not exclusive. A coalition partner on

---

[14] Hamilton, C. and Whalley, J. (1987) "A View from the Developed World", in J. Whalley (ed.), *Dealing with the North: Developing Countries and the Global Trading System*, London, Canada: CSIER, University of Western Ontario, p8.

one issue may not remain a partner on others. The level of organisation of coalitions will also vary and few of the potential coalitions described below are likely to approach the level of institutionalisation found in military alliances, for example. Finally, the coalitions that have been prominent to date in the Uruguay Round of trade negotiations have often been directed towards agenda setting. Their success at the much more difficult task of formulating a common negotiating position remains to be seen.

Each developing country will need to weigh the opportunities and risks presented by possible coalitions that it could join. This study is meant primarily to illuminate both the opportunities and obstacles to a more activist and innovative attitude toward coalition formation.

Southern Bloc on the Sidelines: Trade Negotiations before the Uruguay Round

As Gilbert Winham describes in his account of the Tokyo Round negotiations, the developing countries played a somewhat larger role in those negotiations as compared to their "wholly marginal" participation in the Kennedy Round. Their efforts were, however, concentrated on such exercises as the framework negotiation which was designed to embed preferential status within the GATT regime. Efforts to construct developing country coalitions on more concrete measures, such as tariff reductions, foundered on divisions within the group. While the Latin American countries pushed for preferential tariff cuts, they were opposed by the African states, which resisted a reduction in the preferences that they already received from the EEC.[15]

Three principal explanations can be offered for the peripheral role of the developing countries in past GATT negotiations. First the structure of the negotiations themselves suggested that a relatively passive stance made sense. Trade negotiations, particularly tariff negotiations on a reciprocal basis, do not offer many incentives for smaller economies to participate actively. They have little to offer, since they are not principal suppliers or large markets and, given the extension of MFN status, they could obtain the resulting benefits in any case. Since the developing countries did not accept the principle of

---

[15] Winham, G.R. (1986) *International Trade and the Tokyo Round,* Princeton NJ: Princeton University Press, pp272-7.

reciprocity, incentives for active participation were further diminished. Second, alternative forums for negotiations also beckoned to the third world. Instead of negotiating for benefits with the existing postwar regimes, the G77 sought extensive changes in those regimes through negotiations that included a broad spectrum of issue areas. The negotiations, and the north-south cleavage that they presupposed, also hardened the dominant, southern bloc model of coalition formation. Finally, and related to the appeal of the new international economic order (NIEO), the benefits of liberalisation and non-discrimination in the trading system (two key norms of the GATT regime), were reduced by the strategy of economic development endorsed by many developing countries, particularly the largest ones (China, India and Brazil). Until the 1980s, international trade was viewed, at best, as an ancillary engine of growth by many developing countries. If trade and exports were not critical to economic development, then negotiations within the existing trade regime were bound to receive less attention.

Each of these obstacles to increased participation by the developing countries was lowered, if not removed, during the 1980s. In contrast to the Kennedy and Tokyo Rounds, developing countries were actively involved in the discussions that led to the Uruguay Round. The large number of accessions or requests for accession to GATT, including by such major trading countries as Mexico and China, indicate that the issues on the table are regarded as important by the developing countries. Heightened interest in the latest round of trade negotiations has also been stimulated by the decline of global negotiations and the agenda of the NIEO. The GATT round is one of the few games in town, in large measure because of the hostility of the USA regarding the global negotiations arena. Finally, the economic circumstances of the 1980s have also moved the élites of the developing countries towards greater interest in export expansion and hence the international trade regime. The debt crisis has had a mixed impact (discussed below), forcing import contraction far more than export expansion and lowering the perceived ability of many developing countries to liberalise their commercial policies. The successive shocks of the last decade and pressure from the north have produced an acceptance, sometimes grudging, of more outward oriented policies, although such policies need not include import liberalisation. In shaping the agenda for the Uruguay Round, the new importance of developing country actors was clear, as was the erosion of the previous bloc model of interaction. The coalition model that will dominate during the Uruguay Round remains uncertain, however. There are four basic options, some of which could be combined:

1   In the event that the trade negotiations stall or fail, an accentuation of bilateralism or minilateralism within (or outside) the multilateral GATT framework is likely;

2   A pattern of coalitions across the north-south divide could develop in the Uruguay Round;

3   A looser southern coalition could develop in which the first and second generation newly industrialising countries (NICs) would take a leadership role; or

4   The previous pattern of a broad developing country bloc could be re-established, concentrating its negotiations on questions of regime change and pursuing a joint programme with linkages to other issue areas, such as international finance.

These patterns are dependent not only on perceived developing country interests, but also on the strategies of the major industrialised country participants. They are also highly dependent on the agenda issues in question. As described below, certain issues (such as agriculture) point towards coalition formation across the north-south divide, while others (safeguards) are more likely to produce a predominantly southern coalition. Each strategy has certain benefits and costs for particular groups of developing countries as a result. What follows is an analysis of the clusters and coalition building blocks that might result.

Bilateralism and Minilateralism: A Likely Second Best?

Given the circumstances of the 1980s, and particularly the absence of a dominant economic power, bilateral or minilateral approaches to trade negotiations may be more successful than multilateral negotiations at the Uruguay Round.[16] Certainly such options could grow in importance if current trade negotiations stall or fail. These less-than-multilateral outcomes describe two distinct scenarios. Bilateral or minilateral fragmentation of the GATT system could grow from an accentuation of

---

[16] See Yarbrough, B.V. and Yarbrough, R.M. (1987) "Cooperation in the Liberalization of International Trade: After Hegemony, What?", *International Organization* 41, 1 (Winter), pp. 1-26.

the trend towards managed trade, following such existing models as the Multi-Fibre Arrangement (MFA), or 'grey area' measures of voluntary export restraint (VER). Rather than organised protectionism, a second scenario views these possibilities as a means of preserving and extending islands of liberalisation in a global system tending toward greater closure. The arrangements might be discriminatory but, between partners, greater liberalisation would result. It is worth examining each of these scenarios for its likely impact on developing countries.

A system of managed trade is usually held up as a commercial nightmare for developing economies which will confront their far larger industrialised partners in an unequal contest with little or no international surveillance. The pronounced interest of many developing countries in strengthening certain norms of the GATT multilateral system (at least as applied to OECD countries) suggests that they have sensed this impending nightmare. Yet one could also point to certain sectors - textiles and apparel in particular - that are already intensively managed on a bilateral basis, with little GATT oversight, and which represent considerable successes for developing country exports.

The textiles and apparel case offers substantiation for minority arguments that managed trade between north and south is inevitable and that it need not be disastrous. Considerable evidence exists that any 'new protectionism' directed against the dynamic exporters of the developing world has been ineffectual in restraining the growth of their exports, although on the key question of whether exports would have been significantly higher in the absence of bilateral management, the evidence is mixed.[17] For the NIC, managed trade affords some of the same benefits perceived by the OECD countries - a stable market share protected from more competitive suppliers - as well as offering a substantial portion of the rents. By forcing suppliers into more sophisticated lines of production, it could be argued that such arrangements also provide a beneficial industrial policy for adaptable developing countries.

These short term advantages for some of the NICs may have implications for coalition building in such sectors as textiles, since the

---

[17] See Anjaria, S. I., Kirmani, N. and Peterson, A. B. (1985) *Trade Policy Issues and Developments*, IMF Occasional Paper No. 38, Washington DC: IMF, pp23-4, 81-2 for a review of the literature.

impact of liberalisation in the textiles and apparel sector may be uneven in its benefits. Nevertheless, most developing countries are not convinced of the advantages of a more managed system of trade, with the possible exception of commodities. Even the skilful Asian NICs have discovered that the import competing industries in their major markets are capable of learning as well, and that bilateral regimes can be tightened. For the second and later generation industrialisers, market sharing agreements may temporarily stimulate 'quota seeking' manufacturing exports but, in general, they are particularly damaging for new and more competitive suppliers.

Should the trading environment deteriorate, particularly because of failure at Geneva, another variant of bilateralism and minilateralism could beckon. Developing countries could seek liberalising agreements with industrialised countries or, in an effort to expand south-south trade, with other developing countries. Such arrangements have become a theme of American commercial diplomacy in recent years - for instance, the Caribbean Basin initiative, or proposed free trade agreements with Canada and Israel. The Lomé Convention is an earlier example with roots in colonial ties between European states and the ACP group of developing countries. Developing country preferential trading arrangements have a different lineage. Strongly backed by UNCTAD in the 1960s and 1970s, they have been seen as a means not only of benefiting from economies of scale, but also of increasing the bargaining leverage of developing economies with both the industrialised world and multinational corporations. Few have been very successful at increasing intraregional trade. Most northern observers are sceptical of their benefits, but many developing countries remain impressed by their prospects for market expansion, particularly as a liberalisation 'halfway house' for relatively inefficient manufacturers.[18] Such arrangements pose risks for both the global trading system and for individual developing countries. They could serve as building blocks for a larger, liberalising multilateral system but

---

[18] Sceptical views are given in Mazzeo, D. (ed.) (1984) *African Regional Organizations*, Cambridge: Cambridge University Press and Wolf, M. (1984) "Two-Edged Sword: Demands of Developing Countries and the Trading System" in J.N. Bhagwati and J.G. Ruggie (eds) *Power, Passions and Purpose*, Cambridge, Mass: MIT Press. Several authors in Whalley, J. (ed.) (1987) *Dealing with the North: Developing Countries and the Global Trading System*, London, Canada: CSIER, University of Western Ontario are positive about such arrangements.

preferential agreements could easily become inward looking rather than outward looking. External liberalisation may fail to keep pace with internal freeing of trade; indeed, the latter may distract attention from the importance of the former. In addition, this 'à la carte' approach to trade negotiations and liberalisation produces even greater fragmentation in the world trading system and both a psychological and a real undermining of the MFN principle.[19]

Individual developing countries would have to calculate their long term bargaining advantages within such a bilateral or minilateral relationship and, given the availability of government attention and personnel, the opportunity costs for participation in the global trading arena. Larger developing countries that are highly dependent on particular industrial country markets and that have attractive internal markets to use as a bargaining resource may find bilateral arrangements attractive; Mexico is a possible case in point. For smaller and less diversified economies, even collective bargaining may not yield significant gains; the experience of the ACP states in their bargaining with the EEC provides a caution to other, similar economies.[20]

The popularity of bilateralism and minilateralism as liberalising (rather than management) strategies is likely to be affected by the success or failure of the GATT negotiations. Some fraction of developing country interest in the new trade round derives from a disenchantment with south-south regional trading arrangements. In pursuing an activist course at the multilateral level, however, choice among alternative strategies remains.

North-South Coalitions with Multilateral Negotiations: Common Interests or Cooption?

In the wake of failed efforts at global north-south negotiations, many northern observers have suggested that developing countries form coalitions across the north-south divide if their negotiating goals are to be achieved. Sewell and Zartman, for example argue that,

> ...perhaps the most important single innovation needed in north-south relations is ways and means to develop coalitions

---

[19] On these risks see Hufbauer, G. and Schott, J. J. (1985) *Trading for Growth: The Next Round of Trade Negotiations* Washington, DC: IIE.

[20] See the conclusions of Ravenhill, I. (1985) *Collective Clientelism: The Lomé Conventions and North-South Relations*, New York: Columbia University Press.

between northern and southern countries on various specific
issues without undermining the unity of the Third World.[21]

Arguing the benefits of such coalitions does not produce them,
however. Embarking on this strategy requires an analysis of latent
coalitions that the developing countries might bring into being and a
clear assessment of the risks to southern interests that such a course
poses.

In analysing this alternative, the economic interests of the
developing countries are assumed to determine their behaviour in trade
negotiations. As noted below, ideological or political goals could
incline the third world to a resurrection of the bloc strategy, but here
economic aims are awarded dominance. In examining the
heterogeneous interests of the developing economies in trade
negotiations, several overlapping issue clusters emerge. The principal
groups are:

- Competitive exporters of manufactures (the NICs, the ASEAN
  countries, and other second generation industrialisers);
- Exporters of temperate agricultural products;
- Exporters of other commodities; and
- Those countries with serious international debt repayment
  constraints (indicated by rescheduling).

These clusters may not capture all the divisions within the
developing group, but they highlight certain features that have already
determined the coalition behaviour of some developing countries.
Certain likely alliances across the north-south line become apparent
using these criteria for divisions. Agriculture has already witnessed an
incipient coalition in the Cairns Group, formed in response to the
damaging European-American agricultural subsidies war. The group is
notable in that it includes not only exporters of foodstuffs, north and
south, but also current exporters of tropical commodities who are
concerned over indirect damage to their exports and also have hopes of
future diversification (Malaysia and Indonesia, for example). Two risks

---

[21] Sewell, J.W. and Zartman, I. W. (1984) "Global Negotiations: Path to the Future or
Dead-End Street?" in J.N. Bhagwati and J.G. Ruggie (eds) op cit.

emerge from north-south collaboration on this issue. First, although the EEC agreed to the inclusion of agriculture in the Uruguay Round, it promises to be an issue of major conflict. The experience of the Tokyo Round, in which stalemate over agriculture stalled the talks for four years, could be repeated. A second risk is the opposition of developing countries which have depended on imports of foodstuffs (India, China) or which protect their agricultural sectors (Korea). This potential conflict among developing countries is likely to be reduced by the substantial progress that has been made in China, South Asia and Indonesia in increasing agricultural production. From being substantial importers of foodstuffs, they have, in some cases, become self sufficient and could potentially become exporters.

Outside agriculture and the Cairns Group, north-south coalitions-in-formation are more difficult to discern. For selfish reasons, the USA may support developing country exporters of manufactures in their push for less managed trade, particularly in restraining the use of safeguards. The United States sees an opening of the Japanese and European markets as a means of relieving some of the pressure on its own market from the dynamic exporters of Asia. The USA also has an interest in strengthening the GATT system to avoid a system of managed trade in which it would be at a comparative political disadvantage: as compared to Japan, the USA is relatively inept at managing trade to secure competitive gain.

The developing countries share common interests with Japan in tightening the use of countervailing duties and the definition of subsidies, in circumscribing the use of safeguards, and in strengthening the GATT system, since Japan remains the subject of discriminatory NTBs at the hands of the USA and the Europeans. Smaller industrialised countries, such as Canada and the Nordic countries, would also be interested in this issue. Should resolution of the debt problems of the developing countries be linked to the trade negotiations, Japan could well smooth a resolution through contributing to its financing. With the Europeans there may also be a joint interest in resolving the debt crisis, but, given their lack of enthusiasm so far, it is not clear on what issues the developing countries might form a firm coalition with the EEC. Given Europe's interests in sub-Saharan Africa, commodities might be one such issue but, in general, the African states may be the least involved of the participant developing countries.

Overall, a strategy of seeking alliances and coalitions across the north-south divide could offer gains on particular issues but the risk in this strategy is that the developing countries would find themselves confronting their giant trading counterparts in asymmetric bargaining situations within the coalitions or joining battles, in agriculture for example, that may serve the interests of one or another industrialised country but not their own. Most importantly, the value of concessions made by the developing countries increases if they are made in a coordinated fashion by at least the largest country exporters. This positive value in coordination (and the fact that the more industrialised developing countries have the most to offer in bargaining with the industrialised countries) points to a third strategy.

Leadership by the NICS, for the NICs?

A strategy in which the NICs, the developing countries with the greatest stake in a liberalised trading system, took an active lead in bargaining on behalf of a looser southern coalition is the strategy of choice for most northern observers.[22] This approach concentrates on the common interest of those developing countries seeking more secure access for their manufactures in northern markets, using their own combined internal markets as an inducement.[23] NIC leadership in making a constructive proposal to the OECD would at least put northern protection on the defensive and could achieve reductions in barriers that would benefit less industrialised developing countries as well. The strategy is appealing, but it immediately confronts an important question: which NICs? In fact, two leadership groups emerged in the negotiations preceding the Punte del Este meetings:

• Those resisting the new agenda proposed by the USA, especially Brazil and India; and
• A group (with ASEAN at its core) that was willing to break with the traditional southern stance and support the new round.

---

[22] For example, see Wolf, M. op cit, p222 and Nau, H. (1985) "The NICs in a New Trade Round" in Preeg, E.H. (ed) *Hard Bargaining Ahead*, New Brunswick, NJ: Transaction Books, p78.
[23] For example see Wolf, M. op cit, p212-5; Behrman, J.R. (1984) "Rethinking Global Negotiations: Trade", in J. N. Bhagwati and IG. Ruggie (eds) op cit p248; Hamilton, C. and Whalley, J. (1987) op cit p12-13; Hudec, RE. (1987) *Developing Countries in the GATT Legal System*, London: Macmillan, for TPRC, Part II.

The latter group was apparently supported by several smaller Latin American states and by the Francophone African states. Two groups - the largest Latin American exporters (Brazil and Mexico) and ASEAN - are the hinges of any southern bloc and the likeliest candidates for leadership, given their exporting records, their diversified interests in the negotiations and the size of their domestic markets. Since Brazil opposed the agenda and has been sceptical of the talks, the question of how the principal exporting countries could unify to lead is a pressing one.

A second issue is the outline of a NIC-led strategy. The answer is complicated by the fact that how the developing countries bargain - whether by reciprocal bargaining or not - is one of the issues on the table. Once again, a chorus of northern observers has argued that S&D treatment has meant little of benefit in economic terms (though the benefits have disproportionately accrued to the NICs) and has had the more important political and legal effect of undermining the GATT regime, to the detriment of developing country interests.[24] Although uniform in their assessment, these critics are not in agreement on whether a move toward greater reciprocity or 'graduation' will result in significant gains for the developing countries.

At least three NIC-led bargains seem possible. These are strategies which focus on the constitutional, the instrumental and the substantive. At the constitutional level - dealing with the structure of the trade regime - the NICs could trade a "reasonably specific programme for integrating their trade regimes into the GATT system of open trade and non-discrimination", for a strengthening of the GATT regime in ways desired by the developing countries, particularly in restraining countervailing duties, anti-dumping penalties and safeguard measures, and in strengthening procedures for dispute settlement.[25] Special and differential treatment would be reserved for the poorest developing countries (although they too could be encouraged to liberalise their trade regimes). Such a bargain displays symmetry and, at other levels of bargaining, the knotty question of reciprocity might be circumvented by the same concept or by using the idea of 'unequal reciprocity'.

---

[24] Preeg (1985) op cit p13.

[25] Arguing for Southern participation in negotiations over services, Bhagwati notes in Finger, M.J. and Olechowski, A. (eds) (1987) *The Uruguay Round*, Washington, DC: World Bank, p214, that the Uruguay Round "is unlikely to yield anything more concrete than a code or an agreement of principles".

A second bargain - the instrumental one - would focus on exchanging concessions on quantitative restrictions (QRs) affecting trade in manufactures. For north and south, QRs are perhaps the most salient trade barriers, and certainly are squarely within the existing GATT regime. The NICs could propose that the OECD states commit themselves to a phased elimination of existing QRs affecting manufactures, perhaps including 'grey area' measures. Such a bargain could be coordinated with safeguards negotiations to improve control over the emergence of new, equally restrictive barriers. In return the NICs could offer to bargain over their own QRs on the basis of unequal reciprocity, making concessions clearly smaller in magnitude than those they would receive. For example, they could offer a code that would place some limits on their future use of GATT exceptions permitting the use of QRs for BoP reasons, infant industry promotion and development needs. The proposed limits could be quite loose, but OECD governments might value an agreement that did little more in the short run than establish principles covering NIC markets. NIC governments that would reap most of the benefits of greater market access could consider side deals with neighbours and others in the G77 to obtain their political support.

A third, substantive bargain concerns the sectoral scope of GATT and would probably be the most controversial. The NICs and the other developing countries have been highly sceptical of America's strenuous efforts to bring services into the new round. In fact, all participants seem to have some difficulty estimating their interests in this diffuse set of industries and sectors. While the specific outlines of a services agreement or code remain obscure, the NICs could certainly demand that sectors of interest to them be brought within GATT once again, particularly textiles and apparel. This prospective trade has been rejected by some of the NICs as asymmetric, equating existing violations of GATT rules with the expansion of GATT into uncharted territory highly favourable to the OECD countries. The bargain could be made more attractive for the NICs, however, by emphasising labour intensive services of interest to the developing countries and by designing a graduated (unequally reciprocal) code that would impose

---

[26] Rothstein, R.L. (1979) *Global Bargaining: UNCTAD and the Quest for a New International Economic Order* Princeton NJ: Princeton University Press, pp121-2, 150.

few immediate constraints on the NICs.[26] Given the political interests of either side of this goods-for-services bargain, it would be very difficult to negotiate. NIC unity might be difficult to achieve, given their own mixed interests in the MFA regime and in any future services code.

While NIC leadership may result in bargains that benefit them more than the rest of the developing countries (particularly those whose exports are still overwhelmingly based on a small number of commodities), enough common interests exist between the NICs and these other countries to expect that their interests would not be harmed by such bargaining. The poorest and least industrialised developing countries are not likely to gain very much from reciprocal bargaining; indeed, their gains from the trade negotiations are likely to be small. Phasing out the MFA might help (though it would probably benefit China and India most of all). Negotiations to end tariff escalation on processed raw materials have been on the agenda for some time and linkage to issues of debt and development assistance (considered below) could well be of more interest than commercial issues per se. The NICs, in reserving S&D treatment and attempting to win concessions that would benefit them, would be exercising leadership in the strict sense, giving the less industrialised developing countries the chance of a free ride on their bargaining strengths. But the bargain between the NICs and the other developing countries might not be so one sided; southern unity may still produce benefits in bargaining with the north.

A Unified and Pragmatic South

If northern critics are uniform in their scepticism concerning the gains derived from S&D treatment, they are even more unanimous in their disregard for the bloc strategy that has sought that goal. Robert Rothstein has offered a detailed account of the way in which the developing countries, throughout the NIEO negotiations, maintained a high degree of unity at the cost of bargaining inflexibility and ultimate lack of success.[27] The heterogeneity of the south produced a unity based on ideological principles and the simple addition of one group's demands to those of the others. As Rothstein observes, "procedural unity without substantive unity diminishes the possibility of achieving viable settlements".

---

[27] Rothstein, R.L. (1979) ibid, p196.

The bloc strategy was not irrational, however. It grew out of a particular perception of southern economic weakness and a belief that only through southern unity could negotiating concessions be obtained from the northern countries. That fundamental perception remains to be disproven by the critics. As Hudec declares, the main obstacle to improved market access is lack of economic power on the part of the developing countries. Opposition to demands for protection "requires having enough economic power to create, or threaten, equally important economic interests, in an equally sharp and immediate manner".[28]

If a NIC-led strategy may not amass enough economic power to force concessions from the industrialised countries, one needs to ask whether retaining a framework for coordinating developing country actions would add substantially to developing country leverage. The non-NIC developing countries are likely to add little in a process of reciprocal bargaining, but they do add legitimacy, in the form of universality, to the norms of the trading system and to the claims of the NICs to represent the developing countries. While it is difficult to assess, legitimacy does have value. It is that increment that the NICs should seek to retain in their bargaining on behalf of the other developing countries.

Issue Linkage: Debt and Commodities

The strategies of coalition formation outlined here have been limited to the arena of trade negotiations. For many developing countries in the 1980s, however, other international economic issues have been of equal or greater importance. One of the principal causes of import compression by the developing countries during the 1980s has been persistent BoP crises, aggravated by debt servicing obligations and a decline in external finance. The links between trade and finance have been underlined by the IMF and the World Bank in their calls for open markets in the OECD countries for developing country exports. There are also more specific links to trade negotiations in the phasing of any agreed liberalisation in accord with BoP considerations and the possibility of developing country 'credit' for liberalisation already undertaken in the course of an adjustment programme.

---

[28] Hudec (1987) op cit, p215.

A broader linkage has also been suggested i.e. connecting developing country participation in the Uruguay Round with negotiations directed toward a resolution of the debt crisis. However, one of the divisions between prospective developing country leaders is that of the debt constraint. Latin America has been deeply affected by the debt crisis since 1982, while Asia, with the major exception of the Philippines, has largely been spared. This division suggests a major shortcoming in any attempt at linkage between trade and debt as it fragments the developing countries further. Also, it is not clear that linkage in this case would strengthen the position of the developing countries. The 'debt weapon' could prove as short lived and illusory as the 'oil weapon' of the 1980s. The reverse linkage - from trade to debt - overestimates the bargaining leverage of the developing countries within the trade negotiations.

Although a global negotiation linking debt and trade seems of dubious benefit to the developing countries, two more limited connections between the two issue areas could be put on the table during trade negotiations:

1   Developing countries could ask that unilateral trade liberalisation undertaken during adjustment programmes be accepted as part of their concessions during the trade round; and

2   For those countries under a very tight BoP constraint, international financial assistance could be earmarked (as it has been in the past) to support liberalisation measures that are negotiated.

A second issue area that is more closely tied in its substance to trade is that of commodities. Despite more than a decade of negotiation, the situation confronting commodity producers among the developing countries is as bleak as it has been at any time since the 1930s. The trade round could deal directly with such barriers to processing as tariff escalation and could remove the remaining trade barriers (relatively minor) to commodity exports, but additional effort would be required to link these negotiations to a broader attempt to assist the commodity producers, through an expanded Common Fund for Commodities (CFC) and diversification for markets and products. Here, once again, it is not clear that the developing countries, following any of the strategies outlined above, can reopen the issue on more favourable terms.

Conclusion

While the past experience of the developing countries in trade negotiations provides some hint of their future behaviour, the choices in coalition formation, international and domestic, remain wide and possibilities for surprise, especially for academic observers, are great. Nevertheless, this review does suggest certain practical conclusions for the developing countries as they confront the Uruguay Round.

Two particular problems stare out at those who advocate a more activist stance in trade negotiations. The first is achieving substantive unity, at least among the key trading states (and we have noted the large Latin American economies and ASEAN as focal groups). The possibility for division on issues such as services or debt is great and the other options - disaggregated deal making or a return to an ideological and unprofitable bloc strategy - are likely to offer fewer rewards in bargaining with the industrialised countries. Equally important is the question of representation. Although the largest traders must lead, much of the leadership to this point has come from smaller economies, north and south, which perceive strong national interests in a strengthened multilateral system (Colombia is a case in point). Coupling the realities of economic power with the need for adequate representation is far more difficult for the developing countries than for the industrialised countries, where three trading powers so clearly outweigh the others. In part, the problem could be resolved by existing groups, such as ASEAN, but additional innovation may be required.

In general, among the coalition strategies examined, an NIC-led strategy appears potentially the most rewarding for the developing countries and one that seems to fit best within the existing pattern of (unequal) reciprocal bargaining within GATT. Coalition building across the north-south divide appears promising in certain sectors but problems of coordination in formulating a common negotiating position would probably be greater, and the shared interests outside those sectors weaker. Various bilateral and minilateral alternatives outside the multilateral bargaining could provide the arena for focused bargaining between key trading partners but the advantages appear limited for smaller developing countries, which could offer neither a large internal market nor some strategic benefit to their northern partners. Finally, this menu of coalitional strategies should not exclude maintenance of southern unity on certain issues in which legitimacy provides an additional bargaining resource for the south.

Section 2

JOINING THE GAME, WILLING OR NOT: The Uruguay Round Agreements and the Transition to the WTO

SINGLE UNDERTAKING: FROM TOKYO TO MARRAKESH
Chandrakant Patel

"Single Undertaking: From Tokyo to Marrakesh" is extracted from Single Undertaking, A Straightjacket or Variable Geometry?, *published as T.R.A.D.E. Working Paper 15 by the South Centre. Patel examines the pressures to launch new multilateral trade negotiations soon after the conclusion of the Tokyo Round (1973-79) against a background of shifts in United States trade competitiveness, the institutionalisation of contingent trade protectionist measures in developed countries and the less than satisfactory outcome of the Tokyo Round. He discusses the manoeuvres that led to the scope and structure of the work programme of the Uruguay Round of trade negotiations from 1986, in particular the concept of 'single undertaking' which marks one of the greatest differences between the GATT and the World Trade Organisation (WTO) that came into being as a result of the Uruguay Round. Patel concludes that a virtually non-consensual interpretation of the concept of single undertaking inserted in the draft Final Act of the Uruguay Round in 1999 facilitated the "all or nothing" imposition of the results of the negotiations on developing countries.*

Rationalising a New Round of Multilateral Trade Negotiations

Unbalanced Agenda Setting
Multilateral trade negotiations and their conduct are central to the study and practice of the political economy of international trade. Their outcomes often determine whether countries engage in conflict or cooperation, in diplomacy based or power based relations.

In attempting to explain the rationale of the "grand bargains"[29] of the Uruguay Round variety (a broad agenda embracing traditional and

---

[29] Ostry, Sylvia (2000) "The Uruguay Round North-South Grand Bargain: Implications for Future Negotiations" Lecture at the University of Minnesota, September 2000. See www.utoronto.ca/cis/Minnesota.pdf.

new issues, rule making and institution engineering) as opposed to the limited tariff binding and tariff reduction exercises of earlier rounds, many academics and policy makers have favoured the grand bargains approach, seeing it as improving welfare in the Pareto sense. By permitting issue linkages, tradeoffs and exchanges of concessions that are expected to be self balancing, a broad agenda provides incentives to smaller and weaker trading countries to engage in the multilateral trade negotiations process.[30]

But even if one accepts this rationale for a broad agenda, it begs the question, how broad should it be? The prelude to trade negotiations is the equally important exercise of setting the agenda. This establishes the parameters of a final package and, therefore, is critical in ensuring that the programme of work/agenda undertaken is seen as offering something for everyone.

While acknowledging the practical and political limitations for participants with small delegations and low trade weights, it is nevertheless asserted that these could be offset through coalition building.[31] For these participants, losses are to be addressed through 'side payments' to ensure the stability of the negotiated outcome. In the context of multilateral trade negotiations, side payments may consist of promises of improved market access, unbound commitments of technical assistance, best endeavour special and differential treatment (S&D) measures and longer transition periods. Such side payments, to be sure, are not limited to multilateral trade negotiations. Major trading countries are also creditors and principal shareholders in the major multilateral financial institutions, such as the International Monetary Fund (IMF) and the World Bank. Consequently, the leverage of major trading countries over smaller countries is multiplied and helps explain why the latter generally have limited scope for meaningful participation and tradeoffs in multilateral trade negotiations with broad agendas.

In reality, trade negotiations and agenda setting are driven by domestic priorities and relative trade weights among trading partners. Relatively equally sized economies are more likely to reach cooperative

---

[30] See, for example, Christina L. Davies, "How International Institutions and Issue Linkage Promote Liberalization", paper presented at the Annual Meeting of the American Political Science Association, August-September 2002.

[31] For example, the European Community's efforts to block consideration of their Common Agricultural Policy led to the creation of a single issue coalition, the Cairns Group, which included both developed, and developing countries. It was successful in ensuring that agriculture was included in the Uruguay Round agenda.

solutions, whereas those involving larger countries and smaller ones invariably result in uneven outcomes. Smaller countries often find it very difficult to change or influence unfavourable terms of trade even as the option of retaliation against their trading partners remains mostly notional.

An imbalance in negotiating strengths arising, for example, from such unequal trade relations, would almost invariably result in unbalanced negotiating results. The weaker trading party would usually have to make larger concessions (relative to their capacity to make such concessions) in order to alleviate threats of retaliation from, and the more egregious consequences of protectionism in, the stronger trading partner. Actual trade policy practice shows that dominant trading countries will not behave in a benevolent fashion by providing lower rather than higher levels of trade barriers on the grounds that free trade (as a public good) will engender benefits that outweigh the costs of 'free riding'. Free trade is shown not to be a public good since countries can be readily excluded from its benefits. Even then, free riding continues to be a major preoccupation of the dominant trade players and is among the important reasons for seeking reciprocity.

The case for 'grand bargains' is often cast in terms of the 'bicycle theory', in the absence of a forward momentum provided by new initiatives to liberalise trade in a broad round, there is a risk of falling behind and giving succour to latent protectionist lobbies. Trade policies to address the concerns of import competing lobbies are much easier to deal with because trade restrictive measures are easier to design and are instantaneous in their effect. Those designed to promote exports on the other hand depend not only on market access (and import competing lobbies in export markets) but also on investments to mobilise supply capacities. Export competing lobbies therefore can gain only in the context of reciprocal trade liberalisation.

The conclusion that grand bargains can deliver greater liberalisation is not persuasive, given that much of the liberalisation over the last fifty years took place in an incremental fashion and a significant component of it was autonomous and made contingent on national economic development priorities. The use of the concept of grand bargains in the context of multilateral trade negotiations to push forward greater trade liberalisation, indeed, ignores the fact that, as the United Nations Development Programme (UNDP) has pointed out in a new study,

...benefits of trade openness have been greatly oversold. Deep trade liberalisation cannot be relied on to deliver high economic growth and so does not deserve the high priority it receives in the development strategies pushed by leading multilateral institutions.[32]

Issue Linkage as a Negotiating Device to Maximise Leverage

Linking issues is a well honed technique of international negotiations. In the context of the multilateral trade negotiations, explicit emphasis on linking issues as a negotiating device appears to be a relatively novel approach in making tradeoffs explicit among issues and negotiating areas. As has been argued by Tollison and Willet,[33] many of the highly publicised cases of issue linkages appear to have been motivated by attempts by an individual country or groups of countries to extend their dominant bargaining power in one particular issue area into other areas, so as to achieve maximum advantage from their entire array of international interactions.

The influence of domestic lobbies and considerations - rather than a desire to promote global welfare through free trade - in linking one issue area to other issue areas in trade negotiations can best be seen in the legislative delegation of trade negotiating authority from the United States Congress to the President. The legislative process involves the packaging of issues and areas across a broad spectrum of economic interests and lobbies, for example from free traders to protectionists, and from environmental and labour interests to manufacturing and farming interests. Pursuit of the domestic and foreign trade agenda through negotiations is supported by active enforcement of existing trade legislation, to challenge market access barriers to U.S. Goods and services, protect U.S. intellectual property rights, ensure compliance with telecommunications agreements, and address discriminatory foreign government procurement practices.[34]

---

[32] UNDP (2002) *Making Global Trade Work for People*, New York: UNDP. p32.

[33] Tollison, Robert D. and Thomas D. Willet (1979) "An Economic Theory of Mutually Advantageous Issue Linkage in International Negotiations", in *International Organization* 33, (4): Autumn

[34] Office of the United States Trade Representative, *Identification of Trade Expansion Priorities Pursuant to Executive Order 13116*, 30 April 2001, p. 13, at http://www.ustr.gov/enforcement/super301.pdf. These trade laws include Section 301 of the Trade Act of 1974, Section 182 of the Trade Act of 1974 (commonly known as 'Special 301'), Super 301 (mandated by Executive Order 13116 of March 31, 1999), Section 1377 of the Omnibus Trade and Competitiveness Act of 1988, Title VII (mandated by Executive Order 13116 of March 31, 1999), and various US trade preference programmes.

Dissatisfaction with Tokyo Round Implementation

The 1973-1979 Tokyo Round of multilateral trade negotiations under the General Agreement on Tariffs and Trade (GATT), while yielding important advances in reducing tariffs, was widely regarded as being at best modest in attaining its core objectives in dealing with non-tariff barriers. The Tokyo Round negotiations took place on the understanding that participation in the negotiations was optional and consequently each GATT Contracting Party was free to choose if and when it acceded to any of the negotiated Codes.[35] Consequently, not all GATT Contracting Parties became signatories to the Tokyo Round Codes. Some, mainly developed, countries joined all the Codes. Others joined one or two Codes while many joined none at all. Reasons for the reluctance of many developing countries to accede to the Codes varied but largely revolved around the view that such Codes either did not address or were not relevant to their concerns.

The Subsidies Code, for example, was long on new procedural requirements for countervailing duty investigations but imposed very few disciplines on the use of government subsidies, particularly in the area of agriculture. A more general concern for many was the practice among the major trading countries of negotiating the substance of the Codes among themselves in non-transparent ways and presenting them to other participants on a 'take it or leave it' basis.

Although the United States, during the Tokyo Round, had argued for the introduction of GATT disciplines on trade in agriculture, concerted opposition from the European Community (EC) and a number of others prevented this. As the US agricultural export sector (and later its services, pharmaceutical and high technology industry lobbies) began to mount a concerted drive for the launch of a new round of market liberalisation, pressures also began in GATT for developing

---

[35] Among the Codes negotiated in the Tokyo Round were: a subsidies code; an anti-dumping code; a code on customs valuation; an import licensing code; a standards code; and a government procurement code. In addition, three sectoral agreements were concluded covering trade in civil aircraft, an arrangement on the dairy sector and another regarding bovine meat. Finally, a "Framework for the Conduct of International Trade" that included the 1979 "Enabling Clause" concerning developing countries, a decision on balance of payments measures and an understanding on dispute settlement, were likewise adopted as a result of the Tokyo Round.

countries to assume obligations relating in particular to the Tokyo Round Codes. The shifts in competitive position of the US, due in part from its perceived weaknesses in the areas of its traditional comparative advantage and its emergence as a leader of the high technology and services trade, provided the intellectual underpinning for much of the academic and policy establishment in promoting a new round of multilateral trade negotiations. It was argued that, as a consequence of the loss of comparative advantage in 'sunset' industries, shifts to new 'sunrise' sectors would be accelerated by access to new markets for which new international rules and attendant security would become necessary.

Dealing with Free Riders by 'Levelling' the Playing Field
Among the reasons put forward for the launch of a new round was the widely articulated concern with the 'free rider' phenomenon. This arises from the fact that public goods are non-rival and non-excludable, so that the provision of the good to one individual necessarily entails its provision to, or access by, another and that no one can be excluded from its benefits. Accordingly, in the context of the multilateral trading system, thought by some as possessing the characteristics of a public good, free riders consist of those who secure benefits in excess of the obligations they assume from the core trading precepts such as most favoured nation (MFN) treatment and national treatment. Non-reciprocity and special and differential treatment, in this view of the functioning of the system, create a multi-layered and fragmented range of rights and obligations.

Against this background, the concept of single undertaking provided a neat theoretical instrument to sanitise the trading system of free riders and establish a level playing field through a one-size-fits-all trading regime. By requiring reciprocity of benefits among trading partners through negotiating tradeoffs, a single undertaking approach to multilateral trade negotiations would theoretically allow countries to minimise free riding. In the case of bilateral negotiations, this is done by an appropriate choice of products on which concessions are given and sought. In the case of multilateral trade negotiations, this is done by a suitable choice of products to be exempted from the scope of the negotiations.

However, as Hoekman has observed, nations have been quite successful in minimising free riding even outside the use of single undertaking style multilateral trade negotiations. The wide range of measures adopted by developed countries to circumvent unconditional MFN treatment - a core feature of the GATT/WTO system - together with several derogations and the failure to make S&D operational, has meant that the issue of free riding is in substance and practice much less of a problem than has been asserted.

On the other hand, developing countries' assumption of virtually uncircumscribed MFN obligations has facilitated significant inroads into their domestic markets by foreign players and foreign products. At the same time, free riding by the major primary commodity importers as a result of the decline in commodity terms of trade, together with massive net financial transfers from the developing countries, continues to evade the multilateral trading system and its rules.

Therefore, the elimination of free riders in the global trading system, is dependent not on the use of a single undertaking approach to multilateral trade negotiations, but rather on the application of political will to exclude non-participants from the benefits of the system. Given the economic and political power correlations between developed and developing countries, the former are more likely than the latter to exercise and benefit from exclusionary trade policies, whether within or outside the context of single undertaking multilateral trade negotiations - against non-participants in such negotiations.

Preparing for Multilateral Trade Negotiations: The Run Up to the Uruguay Round[36]

Laying the Basis for a New Round of Multilateral Trade Negotiations
Pressures to initiate a new round of multilateral trade negotiations began soon after the conclusion of the Tokyo Round and revolved around the US' desire to seek additional markets for its services and agricultural exports. At the height of the recession of the early 1980s, there were initiatives in the US Congress pushing for aggressive trade reciprocity, arguing that US markets were fundamentally more open than those of its competitors and that, therefore, the levels of trade protection among the trading partners needed to be brought into rough

---

[36] Much of the discussion that follows draws upon the original analysis and reporting by the South-North Development Monitor (SUNS) and its Chief Editor, Chakravarthi Raghavan, from 1986 to 1994. This remains one of the few authoritative sources of reporting on the "launch, conduct and conclusion" of the Uruguay Round from the perspective of developing countries. See http://www.sunsonline.org.

balance. Concern with free riders, 'fragmentation' of the trading system and the view that the 'playing field was not level' provided further ammunition to both academics and US policymakers to rationalise its essentially market opening objectives.

Developing countries opposed the launch of a new round of multilateral trade negotiations after the Tokyo Round. In early May 1984, Uruguay on behalf of developing countries submitted a joint position paper relating to the improvement of world trade relations through the implementation of the GATT work programme.[37]

The paper underscored the worsening international economic environment for developing countries and the fact that previous rounds of trade negotiations had failed to ensure additional benefits for them.[38] It pointed out that, since the end of the Tokyo Round in 1979, developed countries had intensified the imposition of restrictive trade measures against developing country exports.[39] In opposing the suggestions for a new round of trade negotiations, the paper called for the implementation of past commitments undertaken by developed countries in previous rounds of trade negotiations and for the completion of the 1982 GATT work programme.[40]

However, proposals to launch a new round, also being openly advocated by the then GATT Director General, Arthur Dunkel, received strong support from the report of a group of eminent businesspeople and academics appointed by him in 1984.[41] The near complete advocacy in the Leutwiler Report of the US position on the desirability of a new round and the inclusion of services and other new issues set the stage for the previously divided Organisation for Economic Cooperation and Development (OECD) countries to come out in support of a new round.

The OECD, in early 1985, proposed that a preparatory meeting be convened under GATT to fashion an agenda for the proposed round. However, India, on behalf of a group of twenty four developing

---

[37] GATT document "Uruguay (on behalf of developing countries) Improvement of World Trade Relations Through the Implementation of the Work Program of GATT", L/5647, 4 May 1985.

[38] Ibid, para 1.

[39] Ibid, para 2.

[40] Ibid, para 6.

[41] GATT (1985) *Trade Policies for a Better Future* (The Leutwiler Report).

countries,[42] continued to express reservations about the desirability of a new round.[43] Instead, as a matter of priority, they stressed that confidence-building measures needed to be taken by developed countries, notably with respect to standstill and rollback of protectionist measures that had been enacted and selectively applied against developing countries since the end of the Tokyo Round. They also called for multilateral action on areas of special interest to developing countries, such as textiles and clothing, tropical products, subsidies, countervailing and anti-dumping procedures against developing country exports, safeguard measures, dispute settlement, and S&D.[44]

However, once the Association of Southeast Asian Nations (ASEAN) and a number of Latin American countries came out in qualified support of a new round, things moved very quickly. By November 1985, the GATT Contracting Parties established a Preparatory Committee "to determine the objectives, subject-matter, and modalities for participation in the multilateral trade negotiations".[45] The work conducted in the meetings of the Preparatory Committee ran on essentially two tracks outside the formal GATT structures, with one consisting of key developed countries and a group of developing countries (whose work was jointly sponsored and alternatively chaired by Colombia and Switzerland), and the second consisting of a separate group of ten developing countries.

Expanding the Negotiating Agenda from Goods to Other Areas
The issue that dominated much of the discussions in the preparatory process concerned the desirability of including services on the agenda and, later, modalities for its treatment in the negotiations. For developing countries, including many who were in support of the proposed round, a central concern regarding the inclusion of services in the round was the potential for extracting concessions by linking core trade issues with non-trade issues such as services.

---

[42] These were Argentina, Bangladesh, Brazil, Burma, Cameroon, Colombia, Cuba, Cyprus, Egypt, Ghana, India, Ivory Coast, Jamaica, Nicaragua, Nigeria, Pakistan, Peru, Romania, Sri Lanka, Tanzania, Trinidad and Tobago, Uruguay, Yugoslavia, and Zaire.
[43] GATT, India (on behalf of 23 developing countries) Improvement of World Trade Relations, L/5818, 7 June 1985.
[44] Ibid, para 8:A - C.
[45] *SUNS*, 25 January 1986, at http://www.sunsonline.org.

Unlike the actual physical flow of goods involved in trade in goods, many services and investments tend to be established and provided through a quasi-permanent presence in the host economy. The historical experiences of many developing countries with the deep reach and control of foreign enterprises in virtually every aspect of their polity and economy led most developing countries to strongly resist the inclusion of investment and services on the negotiating agenda. For the proponents of a wider and more ambitious negotiating agenda, on the other hand, concerns regarding culture, history and policies to manage the presence of foreign services providers and investors were no more than disguised non-tariff barriers.

Once the United States and developed countries' agenda prevailed *vis à vis* the launch of a new round of multilateral trade negotiations, the only option left to developing countries was to minimise the damage. This was achieved, in part, through negotiations involving some developing countries and the EC, which for different reasons had reservations about a trade round that embraced liberalisation of agriculture.

The solution that was found revolved around ensuring a clear legal and institutional separation between negotiations on goods, on the one hand, and on services, on the other. Part I of the 1986 Punta del Este Declaration was confined to trade in goods and traditional GATT issues such as tariffs and non-tariff issues, GATT Articles, the Tokyo Round Codes, dispute settlement, safeguards, and subsidies and countervailing measures. The inclusion of Trade Related aspects of Intellectual Property Rights (TRIPS) and Trade Related Investment Measures (TRIMS), while opposed by many developing countries, was circumscribed by placing it in the framework of trade in goods. From the standpoint of developing countries the inclusion of agriculture, tropical products, natural-resource based products, and textiles and clothing in the goods negotiations provided a degree of balance to the agenda, as did the inclusion of provisions on standstill and rollback. Part II of the Declaration concerned services where developing countries also succeeded in ensuring that a multilateral framework on services shall "respect the policy objectives of national laws and regulations applying to services and shall take into account the work of relevant international organizations".[46]

---

[46] Part II, 1986 Punta del Este Declaration.

As noted earlier, Part I:B(ii) of the 1986 Punta del Este Declaration refers to the launch, conduct and implementation of the outcome of the negotiations as a single undertaking. Its placement in the part dealing with trade in goods was to ensure that it would not cover Part II, and hence stress the organic separation of the two negotiating mandates and areas. This separation was to be safeguarded throughout the negotiations by conducting the work on services under a separate negotiating group on services.

Introduction and Use of Single Undertaking in the Uruguay Round
The concept of single undertaking first emerged in the preparatory process for the Uruguay Round at the initiative of the European Community (EC), now the European Union (EU), and was widely seen as a camouflage to protect its core interests in agriculture. But it also received support from a number of other countries, albeit for different reasons. The EC's other preoccupations related to rollback, the balance of rights and obligations (a euphemism for the unfavourable balance of trade against the EC in EC-Japan trade relations) and 'globality' of negotiations. The concept of 'globality' of the negotiations, i.e. the launch of the Uruguay Round as a single political undertaking, was later interpreted by the EC to support the linking of issues in trade in goods with those in trade in services in order to maximise its negotiating leverage over the entire set of negotiations. It also ensured that its concessions were properly 'priced'. This interpretation of issue linkage thus required not only organic linkages between issue areas, but also the totality of negotiations.

The single undertaking concept formalised the strategy of issue linkage but also extended the process to one that bound all the issues and all participants into a single decision. It provided the EC with an instrument to stall and, if necessary, walk away from the negotiations if the package likely to emerge did not meet its expectations. Likewise, by giving each of the participants the right to invoke the device of a single undertaking it provided, at least in theory, the wherewithal to engage in tradeoffs between specific negotiating areas.

A number of developing countries, notably in Latin America, saw single undertaking as an instrument to ensure that the issue of agriculture, in particular, was not side tracked in the negotiations. Earlier efforts to include agriculture in the multilateral trade negotiations had been thwarted by understandings reached between the US and the EC during the Tokyo Round. Single undertaking, therefore, became an important tool to safeguard the globality of the agenda for some developing countries.

The success of a group of Latin American agriculture exporters at the Brussels Ministerial meeting in 1990, in rejecting the compromises reached primarily between industrial countries during and after the Montreal meeting in 1988, suggested that single undertaking was a two edged weapon. Developing countries' refusal to agree to an outcome without satisfactory progress on agriculture represented, arguably, the first time that the notion of linkages and interdependence of issues in the negotiating package on goods was put to practical effect. In asserting their intention to insist on a balance in the negotiations, developing countries signalled that they were prepared to insist on "the conduct of the negotiations as a single undertaking", believing that their negotiating interests would be best served, in the long run, through a single undertaking approach to the negotiations.

Soon after the launch of the Uruguay Round, it became clear that issues of interest to the developed countries appeared to be moving on a faster track than those that were of interest to developing countries. Although the 1986 Punta del Este Declaration provided for a provisional or definitive implementation of any "early harvest" agreements that may be made in the course of the Uruguay Round, the EC reportedly claimed that the only early harvest date of interest to it was the concluding one, i.e. 1990. It, therefore, became necessary for some of the developing countries directly involved in the negotiations to clarify their understanding of the ground rules for the negotiations and of the single undertaking approach.

The then Ambassadors of Brazil and India, in separate statements to the Group of Negotiations on Services (GNS) in February 1987, observed that the launch of the negotiations at Punta del Este was a single political undertaking and as such they were bound by it. The Indian Ambassador then went on to outline four elements as constituting the overarching political globality of the entire Uruguay Round negotiating process - as distinct from the technical and organic globality of the negotiations in goods. These, according to him, were:

1   The unity of time and place for the launch of the Uruguay Round at the 1986 Punta del Este meeting;
2   The establishment of a Trade Negotiations Committee (TNC) to oversee the work of the major negotiating bodies, i.e. the Group of Negotiations on Goods (GNG) and the Group of Negotiations on Services (GNS);

3   The existence of common points of time for the commencement and conclusion of the two distinct processes of negotiations on goods and negotiations on services; and

4   The provision that the decisions on implementation of the outcomes of the negotiations in the two processes would be taken at two separate Ministerial meetings on the pattern of Punta del Este, i.e. a GATT Ministerial Conference for the negotiations on goods, and a separate Ministerial meeting of GATT Contracting Parties for the negotiations on services.

In this interpretation of the concept, there was no presumption that each decision and outcome of the GNG would be binding on each and every GATT Contracting Party. Neither was there any expectation of tradeoffs between the negotiations on goods and negotiations on services. The legal and institutional separation of the GNG and the GNS processes mandated in the 1986 Punta del Este Declaration was expected to prevent any risk of tradeoffs occurring between these two negotiating areas.

At the conclusion of the major part of the negotiations in 1991, the draft Final Act (the Dunkel text) provided for an interpretation of single undertaking that, in effect, required each member to accept the text on each and every subject covered therein. Although refraining from characterising the draft Final Act as an 'all or nothing' text, then GATT Director General, Arthur Dunkel, said in a statement of his "understanding" of the draft Final Act that it offered,

> ...a concrete and comprehensive representation of the final global package of the results of the Uruguay Round" and that "[n]o single element of the Draft Final Act can be considered as agreed till the total package is agreed.[47]

The negotiating strategy outlined by the GATT Secretariat consisted of a four track approach:

1   Intensive negotiations on market access in goods;

2   Negotiations on initial commitments on services;

3   Work to ensure legal conformity; and

---

[47] GATT, "Draft Final Act Embodying the Results of the Uruguay Round of Multilateral *Trade Negotiations*", 20 December 1991.

4   "Work at the level of the TNC with a view to examining whether and if it is possible to adjust the package in certain specific areas".

The fourth track eventually became the basis for the later application of a reverse consensus rule, and clearly indicated that the text of the draft Final Act could no longer be reopened unless the TNC agreed to do so. Effectively, this meant that for developing countries, the draft Dunkel text became the final text of the Final Act. Any amendments and deviations from the Dunkel text would be permitted only on the basis of consensus. The application of reverse consensus as a procedural device consequently precluded most developing countries from meaningful participation in the concluding phase of the negotiations. Accordingly, the Dunkel text, in effect, became a take or leave it proposition. The only instances in which changes in the Dunkel text were made were with respect to areas agreed to by the major industrial countries, for which consensus in the TNC was obtained through negotiating pressure on other (including developing) countries.

Modifications to the draft Final Act text were agreed to between the major trading countries in the interval between the submission of the draft Final Act on 20 December 1991 and its adoption by the TNC on 15 December 1993, for approval by a subsequent GATT Ministerial Conference (in April 1994). This reduced the role and contribution of developing countries to that of interested spectators as the key remaining features of the agreements and their institutional underpinning, i.e. the creation of the WTO endowed with a comprehensive dispute settlement understanding permitting cross sectoral retaliation, were settled between the major developed countries. Shukla aptly describes the shift from GATT to WTO as nothing short of a paradigm transformation of the multilateral trading system.[48]

---

[48] Shukla, S. P. (2000) *From GATT to WTO and Beyond*, World Institute for Development Economics Research Working Paper No.195, Tokyo: United Nations University.

THE OUTCOME OF THE URUGUAY ROUND: AN INITIAL ASSESSMENT (extract)
UNCTAD Secretariat

The Uruguay Round of trade negotiations was concluded with the Marrakesh Agreement in 1994 which set out the terms for the establishment of the World Trade Organisation (WTO) in early 1995. The piece reproduced here is taken from a much longer document that analyses the outcome of the Uruguay Round in detail, including coverage of the main provisions of the WTO Agreement.[49] In line with UNCTAD's mandate, this extract specifically examines the likely impact of the outcome of the Uruguay Round for developing countries. It points to many areas that have indeed become problematic for developing countries under the WTO.

Note: the footnote references are in line with those in the rest of this volume and do not reflect the footnote numbering in the original document.

D. Implications

1. General observations

The WTO Agreement does not establish a minimum number of members or a minimum percentage of world trade as a condition for its entry into force (this contrasts with Article XXVI of GATT 1947 which provided for entry into force upon acceptance by countries accounting for 85 per cent of the total trade of the countries shown in its Annex H). Countries that become WTO members will also remain as contracting parties to the GATT 1947 (and thus bound by two legally distinct sets of multilateral obligations) if they do not withdraw simultaneously from the latter.

2. Increase in levels of obligations and problems of accession

The establishment of the WTO will introduce substantial modifications of relevance for the overall system of trade rights and obligations. Thus, contracting parties to GATT 1947 which become

---

[49] Supporting Papers to the UNCTAD Trade and Development Report, 1994 TDR/14 (Supplement).

members of the WTO will be required to accept all MTAs, incorporated in Annexes 1, 2 and 3 of the WTO Agreement, without any exceptions or reservations, as well as to submit their Schedules of concessions on goods, and of specific sectoral and sub-sectoral concessions with respect to market access and national treatment for trade in services. This would lead to a substantial increase in the scope of obligations for all GATT contracting parties, but developing countries, in particular, will be faced with a dramatic increase in the level of their obligations as most emerge from the Round with a much higher level of tariff bindings, in some cased across-the-board, particularly in agriculture, and have accepted new obligations flowing from the revised Tokyo Round Codes,[50] which had previously been accepted by a minority of developing countries, as well as new obligations in the areas of trade in services and, in particular, intellectual property rights. The very strict conditions for accession to the WTO will therefore be a serious challenge to them. The WTO will substantially reduce the flexibility which developing countries have enjoyed under the multilateral trading system with respect to their trade policies and in certain areas considered to fall in the domestic policy sphere. These obligations are somewhat mitigated by the provisions on differential and more favourable treatment, which offer even greater flexibility to the least developed countries.

In addition, the WTO Agreement eliminates the possibility for those developing countries and territories which apply de facto GATT rules in their foreign trade to accede, as is now the case, by a simple declaration under GATT Article XXVI:5 (c).[51] The process of accession will also be much more difficult, including for those developing countries and economies in transition now negotiating their terms of accession to GATT, as they will need to adapt to the new agreements negotiated in the Uruguay Round. For example, they will have to negotiate an "entry fee" on both goods and services, accept a variety of

---

[50] As of May 1994, 15 developing countries were parties to the Agreement on Technical Barriers to Trade; 2 to the Agreement on Government Procurement; 13 to the Subsidies Code; 11 to the Anti-Dumping Code; 12 to the Customs Valuation Code; 12 to the Agreement on Import Licensing; 2 to the Civil Aircraft Agreement; 10 to the International Bovine Meat Arrangement and 4 to the International Dairy Agreement.

[51] These countries were formerly colonies or dependent territories. At present, there are still 13 developing countries and territories in this category.

Agreements that until now have been optional (i.e. most Tokyo Round Codes as revised), and commit themselves to a set of new multilateral rules and disciplines in the areas of agriculture, subsidies, and intellectual property rights, among others.

3. Cross-sectoral retaliation

The WTO foresees, through its dispute settlement mechanism, "cross-sectoral retaliation" between market access concessions and rule-making obligations in the area of goods and new obligations in the areas of intellectual property and trade in services, as well as any new areas for which members decide to negotiate multilateral obligations.[52] Cross-sectoral retaliation, under the Agreement (TRIPs and services), may be authorized under the Understanding of Rules and Procedures Governing the Settlement of Disputes, although procedural devices determine that this would arise only as a last resort. Cross-sectoral retaliation was a major objective of major trading countries; the extent to which it could have positive aspects in defending weaker countries' positions will have to be seen in practice.

4. *Plurilateral Trade Agreements*

Annex 4 of the WTO Agreement "Plurilateral Trade Agreements", while originally intended to provide legal cover for the Tokyo Round Codes not renegotiated in the Uruguay Round, including those applied on a "conditional" MFN basis among signatories, could imply the creation of a legal mechanism for negotiating future multilateral trade agreements of limited membership. The possibility is provided for in relation to the addition of a new PTA to Annex 4 although this must be decided by the Ministerial Conference exclusively by consensus. However, there are no specific rules dealing with the initiation of such plurilateral negotiations.

The possible proliferation of PTAs would limit the application of unconditional MFN and non-discrimination in the international trading system, since they would create rights and obligations only for members that accepted them. Annex 4 could eventually be used as a legal justification to negotiate new agreements among a few members of the WTO, the benefits of which would not need to be extended to

---

[52] See, for example, "President Clinton's submission to Congress of documents concerning the Uruguay Round Agreement, December 15, 1993", *International Trade Reporter*, Vol 10, Washington D.C., 22 December 1993, p. 2164.

other members. It should be noted that the WTO Agreement does not contain an unconditional most-favoured-nation clause, which has instead been included respectively in GATT 1994, GATS and the TRIPS Agreement.

PTAs could eventually be adopted in cases where multilateral negotiations do not lead to consensus among all WTO members, paving the way for individual WTO Member countries with likeminded positions to legalize their relations on specific trade issues under the coverage of the WTO. There are already candidates for future PTAs such as the Multilateral Steel Agreement (MSA), as well as the proposed new agreement covering antitrust issues.[53] Paradoxically, PTAs could lead to a further fragmentation of the multilateral trading system, creating within one organisation different levels of rights and obligations as well as two categories of members.

41ST SESSION OF THE UNCTAD TRADE AND DEVELOPMENT BOARD, 1994 (extract)
UNCTAD Secretariat

The following extract comes from the report of the 41st Session of the UNCTAD Trade and Development Board.[54] The speaker reported covers four areas in which developing countries will have difficulty coping with a more stringent multilateral trading system and suggests a need for more compensatory mechanisms to facilitate the inclusion of such countries in the system.

Chapter IV

ANALYSIS AND ASSESSMENT OF THE OUTCOME OF THE URUGUAY ROUND, IN PARTICULAR IN AREAS OF CONCERN TO DEVELOPING COUNTRIES AND ECONOMIES IN TRANSITION CONCRENED, AND ITS IMPACT ON THE INTERNATIONAL TRADING SYSTEM AND PROBLEMS OF IMPLEMENTATION

211.   The Officer-in-Charge of the International Trade Division, in his introductory statement, drew attention to the initial assessment of

---

[53] See "Draft International Antitrust Code as a GATT-MTO Plurilateral Trade Agreement". International Antitrust Code Working Group, Munich, Germany, July 1993.
[54] UNCTAD Report TD/B/41(1).14 (Vol II).

the Uruguay Round results in the Trade and Development Report 1994 and Supporting Papers and identified four themes in order to assist the Board in structuring its deliberations. First, the WTO Agreement dramatically increased the multilateral trade obligations of developing countries. It also deepened these obligations by establishing disciplines in areas previously considered the domain of domestic policy. However, more specific contractual provisions for differential and more favourable treatment provided developing countries with a certain amount of time-bound flexibility. Their development strategies and trade policies would nevertheless have to be adapted to the post-Uruguay Round system. Under these circumstances, it must be asked to what extent developing countries would be able to emulate the success stories of certain countries, particularly those in the Asian region. Second, tighter multilateral disciplines, combined with a streamlined dispute settlement system, provided new scope for action against trade-restrictive practices and shielded countries from bilateral pressures. It was therefore important to determine the institutional and financial capacity of developing countries to assert and defend their rights effectively within what promised to be a more legalistic, litigious system. Third, the LDCs and many less advanced developing countries could find it extremely difficult to complete in a more liberal trading system. They would also face considerable problems in assuming the burden of their new, more stringent multilateral obligations. The transitional adjustment costs (such as erosion of preferences and higher food prices) would pose a particularly onerous challenge for them. The Trade and Development Report suggested that the international community should consider how such countries could benefit from a "safety net", which should assist them in dealing with adjustment problems, in acquiring improved capacities to compete in international trade, and in making full use of their rights. A Ministerial Decision adopted at Marrakesh on "Measures concerning the possible negative effects of the reform programme on least developed and net food-importing developing countries" constituted a first step in addressing some of these problems. The Board might therefore wish to give priority consideration to the wide range of these countries' special needs in the post-Uruguay Round system. A fourth theme related to the future trade agenda. The Multilateral Agreements themselves contained a built-in agenda for future negotiations. In addition, a variety of other issues, some of which had wider economic, social and political implications, had been suggested at Marrakesh. A preliminary consideration of new and emerging issues would contribute to a better understanding of these issues, including their developmental implications, in view of the Board's forthcoming executive session devoted to this subject.

212.   In conclusion, UNCTAD IX would inevitably have to address the full spectrum of trade issues in the post-Uruguay Round era. The Board's deliberations on this item could also provide policy guidance and focus for the work of the Board leading up to UNCTAD IX.

THE WTO DISPUTE SETTLEMENT SYSTEM
Magda Shahin

"The WTO Dispute Settlement System" is extracted from Magda Shahin's book From Marrakesh to Singapore: The WTO and Developing Countries.[55] *Developing countries were seen as gaining ground from the establishment of the WTO as a rules based system. The enforcement of this system is through the WTO's Dispute Settlement Understanding (DSU). In this extract, Shahin questions the extent to which small and weak countries will be able to utilise the DSU in the absence of any 'credible threat' to those who choose not to comply with the system.*

It is widely believed that the main gain for developing countries from the WTO is a strong rule based system to safeguard their interests. Whether this is accurate or not is still to be seen. Nevertheless, at this point one can advance some basic arguments to consider the extent of the effectiveness of the Dispute Settlement System (DS) within the WTO.

The GATT/DS has been characterised in the past as ineffective. Critics have centred their complaints essentially on three points:

1   The ineffectiveness of the DS in the GATT was often attributed to the 'consensus' rule, which operated at the three levels of establishment of the panel, adoption of the panel report and

---

[55] Shahin, M. (1996) *From Marrakesh to Singapore: The WTO and Developing Countries*, Penang: Third World Network, p22-27.

adoption of countermeasures as a last resort, and could be blocked by either party at any one of these stages;

2   The time taken in the procedures; and

3   Lack of transparency, where the panel procedures remained confidential, even after the adoption of the panel's report.

The Thrust of the DS System

A number of questions were raised by very competent and experienced people working in the system, which I am simply going to reiterate in this context to be able to make a preliminary judgement on the functioning of the system in general. These are as follows:

- Who is the DS favouring? According to the 'Bargaining Power Theory', when negotiations stop, DS starts. In the negotiations, bargaining power is dominant. In the dispute settlement, power becomes irrelevant as the legal considerations become the dominant factor. The DS is supposed to be fair and legal, thus disfavouring power politics to the benefit of the weakest partner, i.e. the developing countries, and thus safeguarding their rights.

- Did the system provide the appropriate incentives to persuade players to use the multilateral context? Did it truly provide a rules oriented system to the society, where all play fair, or does it work on the basis of a dominant hegemony? The second option should be discarded on factual grounds. If the first option is factually correct, what is needed for this option to work? The notion of 'credible threat' in the game theory comes to mind. Is there such a notion in the GATT/DS the role of remedies?

Anyway, whether the system will really be resorted to depends to a large extent on two main points:

1   How the Appellate Body is going to react to the panel decisions; and

2   What will happen if the more powerful country in a dispute does not abide by the panel rulings?

There is nothing in the system that forces the strong country to adhere except moral obligations. Though the disputing party is certainly allowed to impose sanctions, there is no Security Council Chapter 7 in the WTO, which would allow the international community to take any kind of common action and this would be the only type of effective sanctions against a larger or more powerful country which did not implement the panel rulings. There is, however, what is known as 'cross-retaliation'. But it would certainly be wise to think about whose interest such a course of action would serve. Certainly it is the country that has the leverage to use it which would gain the most. China could, but what about a country like Egypt or an even smaller one against the US, the EU or even Japan? Considering this, one may question the validity of the implied threat within the system.

Assessment of the WTO/DS System

To repeat basic arguments put forward by legally competent people in the WTO, let me state the following:

- The consensus rule has been changed, from consensus to negative consensus. Article 6 says, "...unless the Dispute Settlement Body (DSB) decides by consensus not to establish a panel". Negative consensus at all three levels would make implementation easier as there can be no blockage.

- In addition, easier access to countermeasures is provided for through the possibility of cross retaliation. But it remains doubtful that developing countries really have the leverage to use cross retaliation and it might even entail a higher risk as it can be easily used against them. Though cross retaliation has, to a large extent, been disciplined, in that one cannot go from one sector to the other unless all possibilities have been exhausted in the one area and then in the sector itself, it is nevertheless a very strong tool for sanctions in the hands of the stronger countries.

  A very pertinent question that has been raised is whether the hurdle of dispute settlement has just been moved one step further - from refusal to adopt panel reports to refusal to comply in the absence of any credible threat. The answer to this question will only emerge with time and experience.

- Strict deadlines now are well in place. These are six months for normal procedures, possibly extended up to nine, and three months for urgent cases, mainly for food that can go bad.

- The Appellate Body has been established. Its mandate is strictly confined to the examination of the legal part of the dispute.

It is argued that the WTO Dispute Settlement Understanding (DSU) takes care of some procedural impediments without addressing the substance of the problem, namely the establishment of a credible threat in the system equal to that contained in Chapter 7 in the Security Council.

Future practice is awaited with a lot of interest. But future practice might take place in the context of the 'Dole proposal' or of the creation of the Legal Office in 1986 and the reasons behind its creation. Does history repeat itself?

Nevertheless, the overwhelming majority emphasises that the WTO has strengthened the scope of rule oriented policies to the detriment of the power politics which was frequently applied in the past. It is also argued that, while developing countries have very small retaliatory possibilities in trade in goods, their leverage is more pronounced in the area of services and TRIPs. Cross retaliation basically means that a country can suspend its obligations for a certain period of time, for example, by ceasing to protect the intellectual property of or temporarily closing the market to foreign services. But then the question arises, how would a developing country's own economy be affected by such a move?

Although the WTO/DS seems generally to have attracted more praise than criticism, it is the apparent positive points, such as its automaticity and the so called 'binding' nature of its mechanism (which is certainly debatable, as I have tried to show) that attract the most criticism from the US. The risk that decisions could be handed down by representatives of small countries and third world countries sitting in judgement over US actions puts in doubt the US' future compliance.

Parties to a disagreement cannot block the panel's findings, as they could have done under the GATT. The losing side can appeal, and the Appellate Body's ruling is final. It is still to be seen whether the DS is the new teeth of the WTO.

The question will remain, however, whether the purpose of the WTO is to act as the international police, or as an 'enforcement mechanism' or whether it is primarily a negotiating and dispute resolution forum. The latter has proven effective in a number of cases, such as the first dispute case brought to the WTO between two friendly developing countries Singapore and Malaysia. The case was brought to the WTO by Singapore but was settled outside its framework. The US complaint against South Korea's use of shelf life regulations to limit packaged food imports was also settled outside the WTO framework and the US/Japan automobile case was settled in the same manner.

It may be an argument in favour of the system, to say that 1995 saw an increasing involvement of developing countries in the WTO dispute settlement processes. In total, about 50 percent of the cases brought to the DSU were initiated by developing countries.

A major point would be for the WTO to strengthen technical assistance to developing countries in this domain with a view to showing its good faith in enabling the developing countries to use the system and profit from it. In addition, developing countries themselves should aim at strengthening their national capacity in this respect, as the Dispute Settlement Mechanism will remain a key to their integration in the multilateral trading system and to their becoming active players using their rights as well as discharging their obligations.

DID URUGUAY ROUND RESOLVE ANYTHING?
Chakravarthi Raghavan

"Did Uruguay Round Resolve Anything?" was originally published in the South-North Development Monitor (SUNS) *of 14 February 1994. Following on from Magda Shahin's piece (above), Raghavan looks at an actual case of the powerful simply bending or ignoring the rules that are supposed to protect those who are not powerful. The Marrakesh Agreement was drawn up on the assumption of good faith of all the signatories but the US, as it did throughout the GATT era, continues to act unilaterally within a supposedly multilateral system.*

The planned moves of the United States for unilateral trade sanctions against Japan for failure to open up its goods and services markets to US exports will figure prominently this week at the GATT when the Council undertakes the periodic review of US Trade Policy.

The US arguments and explanations that Japan has much less of an import penetration than the US or the EC or that the Japanese market is privately organised to discourage imports and that the Japanese do not change their 'mores', and that the US actions are aimed at opening Japanese markets on an MFN basis, may make the US actions sound almost altruistic. But it does not change the basic thrust of US policy which is one of being above the law.

The timing of the TPRM review now, after the conclusion of the Uruguay Round, with its promises of a 'new trade order' and a strengthened multilateral trading system, brings to the fore the question of how far the US is ready to comply with the law that it wants to lay down for the rest of the world.

While, technically, it could be argued that the US threats and proposed actions against Japan are to be judged in terms of the current GATT and GATT law (which in the US, being a provisional agreement, cannot be cited in domestic courts), the US move, just two months after the adoption of the Uruguay Round texts as a package, will hardly reassure its trading partners that it is likely to change its behaviour in the future. If anything, it will strengthen the view that the present US administration is hard nosed in pursuit of 'mercantilism' and using neo-mercantalist instruments for the benefit of its TNCs and their profits. It will also bring home to groups in developing countries, critical of the Round and its consequences for them, that the 'free trade theology' of the GATT or the future WTO is one that will be preached to the weak but will not practiced by, and cannot be enforced against, the strong.

When the Uruguay Round negotiations were concluded just two months ago there was a great deal of self congratulation by negotiators and the GATT chief Peter Sutherland about the rule based system and the new trade order that will emerge.

A rule based system may not be Dicey's "Rule of Law" but implies that, under it, the 'rules' will be clear, that adherence to rules by signatory governments will be the norm, that the rules will be the same between the weak and strong and that the certainty of remedies and enforcement of rights of the weak will deter violations of the rules.

The GATT was founded in 1947 to counter the inter-war years of bilateral trade diplomacy, agreements and conflicts through multilateralism. And the WTO, with the GATT 1994 annexed, is supposed to enshrine these at a higher level of commitment and obligation in international law by making the WTO a definitive international treaty, unlike the provisional nature of GATT 1947.

Throughout the Uruguay Round negotiations, when the US was holding and threatening to use the panoply of its retaliatory legislations - S.301, Special 301, and the Super 301 (which expired, but which President Clinton now wants to put in place by an Executive Order) - a common refrain was that, once the rules are laid down clearly and issues like TRIPS etc. were resolved multilaterally through rules, the US would no longer use these instruments nor need to have them.

During the six years of negotiations, the US, despite the standstill commitments in the Punta del Este mandate, used its unilateral trade sanctions threats to force many countries to yield ahead of the conclusion of the TRIPS negotiations in the Round - something that the mandate specifically forbade. When some refused to yield, the US took action in the form of denial of duty free access under its GSP schemes. This access has been viewed as a privilege and not a contractual right, and hence not open to dispute settlement, in the GATT but even this is a view that some still challenge.

In the final stages of the negotiations, the idea of a Multilateral Trade Organisation, which was not in the mandate of Punta del Este, was brought in by stretching to breaking point the mandate for improving the 'functioning of the GATT system'. Tied to it was the requirement that participants in the Round must sign the agreements as a package. All this was discussed and negotiated among a few and sprung on all the participants.

The developing countries, in fact, became the most vocal advocates of the MTO (renamed at the last moment as the WTO), arguing that its emergence as an international treaty to which the US would have to subscribe, and provision for a quasi-judicial dispute settlement system, would provide them, as the weak trading partners, a fundamental protection against unilateralism within the trading system. But the US unilateral threats against Japan must now raise questions about this.

Some GATT sources argue that the US is able to threaten and/or take action now because there is no WTO and its annexed agreements in force but things will be different under the WTO. But this is to assume that the US propensity for exercise of unilateral power or pursuit of neo-mercantalist trade policies and instruments will be cured when the WTO comes into being and that, when the Uruguay Round agreements and the WTO enter into force on 1 January 1995, the US will, overnight, become a good citizen and cease to use, or threaten the use of, unilateral trade instruments.

All international treaties are based on the concept in Art XXVI of the Vienna Law of Treaties that an international treaty involves "free consent, good faith and full implementation".

During the negotiations in the Lacarte group on the MTO, the group was advised that the US 'subscribes' to the Vienna Law of Treaties but has not ratified it.

When the MTO/WTO text was being negotiated in that group, a crucial issue related to Art XVI:4. The draft text, agreed in mid November 1993, provided that "Members shall ensure the conformity of their laws, regulations and administrative procedures with the provisions of the annexed agreement". The term "with the provisions" was changed in the final version to "its obligations".

But behind all the arguments about compliance with the WTO agreement and annexes was the assumption that the US government would be acting in 'good faith', would abide by the WTO and its annexed agreements, and would ensure conformity of its "laws, regulations and administrative procedures" with its obligations.

It was also based on the assurances of US negotiators that, while it might be difficult for the Congress to formally take off the statute books the various 301 provisions, there would be neither a need to invoke them nor would the US have recourse to them. The US moves now would put these assurances into question.

US officials have also been publicly saying that the US would not give up its unilateral right to act, whether to advance its trade interests or its view about protection of the environment, so long as there is no GATT or WTO provisions to deal with them and settle disputes. While State Department Official, Timothy Wirth, made such an assertion in testimony before Congress, President Clinton, US trade officials and others have made no secret either of their intentions in public statements or in press briefings.

All this would imply that in the future too, the US might just prefix 'trade related' to any one of its concerns and arguing that these are not covered by the WTO, nor is there an agreement to negotiate them, would entitle it to take unilateral sanctions.

There is probably considerable strength in the argument that, in the future, any trade restrictive or retaliatory measure against a WTO member would be feasible and legal only after the US gets a ruling in its favour under the DSU and gets the sanction of the WTO for the retaliation. And, whether the US seeks prior consent or not, if it acts without consent and thus in violation of the DSU procedures, that itself would become a ground for a complaint and any aggrieved country could haul the US before the WTO and its Dispute Settlement mechanisms.

However, it is not quite clear whether this course of action for an aggrieved WTO member against the US would arise only after a measure is put into force, or even on the basis of a law on the US statute books or a US 'threat' to use that law. And while the WTO and its DSU proceeds on the basis that the rulings should be implemented, if the US chooses not to, then the only remedy is for the aggrieved party to 'retaliate'.

In invoking or threatening trade sanctions, the US proceeds on a different logic and on the basis that, if it announces a long list of trade measures it is contemplating against a country, putting off for some months the actual measure it will pick out of the list, all the trade interests in that country likely to be affected will run up to their capital to pressure their government to settle the problem and not allow the trade insecurity to continue.

It is possible that, in a future WTO with a virtually automatic dispute settlement system, the insecurity caused to a country's trade by such threats might be viewed by a panel as a violation. But this is, at best, an arguable issue and one that could evolve in the long run into GATT law, after at least more than a decade or two of disputes and precedents, and slow the attempts of panels to expand their jurisdiction. It will not provide the kind of trade 'security' and 'climate' where investors will rush in and set up production and export.

FULL PARTICIPATION AND EFFICIENCY IN NEGOTIATIONS
Bhagirath Lal Das

"Full Participation and Efficiency in Negotiations" was originally published in the South-North *Development Monitor (SUNS) 4582 of 12 January 2000. The writer looks at the way in which negotiations were being carried out in the WTO in 2000, and had been for most of the GATT period. He notes the increasing understanding of some developing countries which is changing their negotiating aims and capacity. Das suggests a number of methods for making WTO negotiations more inclusive without sacrificing efficiency.*

In the current WTO system, the various stages of negotiation on a particular subject are: tabling of the proposal by a country in a formal meeting, discussions and negotiations in small group meetings, brief information on the progress given at formal meetings from time to time by the Chair and, finally, when an agreement is reached in the small group negotiations, tabling of the results in the formal meeting for approval.

In this way, countries in general get involved at the initial stage and the final stage, but are almost totally out of the picture in the actual process of the negotiation in the small groups. The small group of countries for negotiation is selected on an ad hoc basis by the Chair of the Council/Committee with the active support of the Secretariat. In practice, the Chair generally depends on the Secretariat for the selection and informal invitation.

Most of the time, almost all the developed countries are in this small group. The presence of the EC ensures the representation of the fifteen countries in the EU. Among the developing countries, generally five to ten are selected, mostly those countries that actively participate in the WTO meetings. They prepare and speak. Sometimes, some others may also be invited if the Chair and the Secretariat fear that they may block the decision in the final meeting if they are not associated in the small group negotiations.

Another parallel or supplementary process in the GATT/WTO system is that of negotiations in selected missions or over lunches and dinners arranged and hosted by the countries that have placed the initial proposal or are deeply interested in the subject. The selection of the countries for such events is, naturally, done by the host mission.

This system has been going on for a very long time, almost since the beginning of the GATT. Though there was some dissatisfaction among the developing countries, there was rarely any formal protest. But the situation after the Uruguay Round has reflected a process of change:

- In the past, very few among the developing countries had the requisite expertise and resources to participate effectively in detailed negotiations but several developing countries have now strengthened their capacity in the capitals and in Geneva to participate in the negotiations;
- Then the risks were low, as the developing countries were not called upon to undertake substantial obligations, however, the character and content of the negotiations have changed in the last ten to fifteen years;
- Previously, the developing countries were mainly negotiating to get concessions from the developed countries whereas, now, the negotiations are focused mainly on developing countries making concessions and the developing countries, rightly, feel that they have to be actively involved in these negotiations, as the

obligations emerging out of the negotiations will be binding on all;

• Industry and trade in the developing countries are becoming aware of the impact of the Uruguay Round results on them and putting pressure on their governments to expand their opportunities; and

• A new feature emerging after the Uruguay Round is the vigil of NGOs, the media and intellectuals in the developing countries on the role of their governments in the WTO negotiations.

The obvious answer is to involve all countries in the negotiations but there are severe practical problems. The process of a multilateral negotiation is complex. When a subject is selected for negotiation, the countries that are interested express their points of interest and concern. These presentations are often extreme at this stage. After the talks proceed for some time, the main interested parties are able to assess the serious interests and objections of other parties.

Some country then puts up a formal proposal in the form of a text, if this had not been done earlier. There are preliminary comments on the text. Some other countries may feel inclined to put their own texts, which may be aligned or opposed to the earlier text. Then all these texts are taken up for consideration. It is at this stage that intense negotiations start on the specific texts.

After a series of negotiating sessions, the duration depending on the seriousness of the subject and the extent of differences, the Chair conducting the negotiations sometimes puts forward their own text in which they try to incorporate the main concerns of all the parties. Points of severe differences and alternatives are put in square brackets. The Chairperson's text is expected to facilitate the process by focusing the negotiation on one paper. Serious negotiations then follow on the basis of this paper. The objective is to narrow down the differences and to accommodate the main concerns of all the interested parties.

Finally, if possible, an agreed text is formulated which is the result of the give and take by all parties participating in the negotiation.

One can clearly appreciate the problem in the direct and active participation of all the one hundred or so WTO Members present in Geneva at all stages of this negotiating process. Particularly when the texts for negotiations start emerging, it will be difficult to reshape them in large gatherings. Therein lies the problem of efficiency in the multilateral negotiations. But the WTO has reached a stage at which the major participants can no longer aspire to give weight only to efficiency, totally ignoring the need for full participation by the entire membership. While seeking efficiency in the process, it is important that full opportunity is given for the active participation of at least the countries that are present in Geneva. Thus the problem can be reduced to finding an appropriate mix of efficiency and full participation in the negotiating process.

It is unlikely that any agreed text will emerge with all the countries directly considering it in a big conference hall. At the same time, it is also necessary that all the countries are fully satisfied that their interests are taken on board and they have had a full say in the emerging texts. In the present greenroom process, the countries that are not present there naturally feel that they did not have this opportunity. Though some countries present may have similar views and interests to theirs, there is no delegated authority to these people to negotiate on behalf of others.

A possible solution could be to form a representative negotiating group. It should consist of a prescribed and small group of negotiators who would be negotiating on behalf of a set of countries. They should be selected jointly by the countries that they will be representing. Thus, these negotiators will not be negotiating for their own respective countries but for all the countries that have selected them. Naturally, the negotiator's own country will be in the group that selects them.

A negotiator in this group will be given the brief for the negotiation jointly by the group of countries that selects them. They will come back to the group for a fresh brief if any concession beyond the earlier brief is to be made in the negotiations. This process will involve frequent meetings of these groups and, in special circumstances, like a Ministerial Meeting, groups may have to be continuously on call so that a negotiator is able to keep their group fully informed on the latest developments in the negotiation and the group is able to give further instructions to the negotiator.

One important precondition for such a process is that the countries in a group have a common, or nearly common, interest and stand on the issues involved in the negotiation. This, in turn, requires two steps. Firstly, groups should be formed in such a manner that countries having similar or nearly similar interests are in one group. Secondly, there will need to be initial consultation and negotiation within a group to hammer out a common stand on the issues in the negotiation. The second step will be a dynamic process in the sense that the common stand of the group will undergo changes and will evolve during the process of the negotiation, depending on the stand and responses of the other groups.

The main problem is how the groups should be formed. One general differentiation could be that there are three broad group clusters, viz, the developed countries, the developing countries and the countries in transition. Considering the number of countries in the current membership of the WTO, there should be three developed country representatives, twelve from the developing countries and one from the transition economies. The developed countries could be divided into three groups, each having one negotiator. Similarly the developing countries may divide themselves into a number of groups, depending on their commonality of interest, each being represented by one or more negotiators.

There are various possible methods for formation of groups among the developed countries and also among the developing countries. The latter may have more problems because of the large numbers involved. But, once a decision is taken in principle to have the groups, the actual formation may not prove to be an impossible exercise. The simplest, of course, would be to form the groups on a stable basis, even though there may be some divergences in relative interests among the countries of a group in different areas. An alternative might be the formation of groups for each subject separately. Though appearing more logical, this may be too cumbersome a process, as groups will have to be formed each time a new subject comes up for negotiation.

It should be noted that this structure is not like the proposal for a Security Council type institution in the WTO which has sometimes been made by some major developed countries. The members of the Security Council speak on behalf of their respective countries whereas, in the structure proposed here, the negotiators will be speaking on behalf of the countries that have selected them. Also the negotiators will be acting under the joint instruction of these countries and will be answerable to them.

Also, this proposed structure is not like the group system that operated in the UNCTAD negotiations. There, the groups among the developing countries were rigidly formed based on their geographical location. In the proposed structure, the formation of the groups is being suggested on the basis of perception of common interests.

Three main points might be raised against this structure

1   It may be feared that it will politicise the WTO negotiations. But an institution like the WTO, which handles the rights and obligations of countries in some important economic sectors, is bound to have an innate political overtone howsoever one may wish to keep it immune from politics. In fact, recognition of this reality, and encouragement of interaction among countries and groups with full realisation of this inevitable feature, will help the institution to proceed smoothly on its path.

2   It might be argued that each country has its own interest in the WTO, and thus it will be unrealistic to think that such a group system will work. With all the individual approaches of the countries in the WTO, it has often been noticed that there are converging interests, and thus the possibility of the group approach should not appear impractical.

3   It may be pointed out that the interests in many areas cut across the divide of developed and developing countries. Thus, to have separate group clusters of developed and developing countries will not be correct. This argument has a lot of force in it. Some countries that are grouped as developing countries at present, may have their interests more aligned to those of the developed countries on most subjects. Similarly there are some areas, like agriculture, where there is an interest group at present which includes both developed and developing countries. Considering these exceptional situations, there may be a need for some adjustment and flexibility in the process of group formation, particularly in the beginning.

But more than these technical points, the real opposition to any such suggestion will come from the major developed countries which have always tried to lead and shape the negotiations according to their own desires. Generally they have found the present system to serve their interests. Hence, they may be totally opposed to any new initiative to change the current negotiating process.

But this would be a short term view. A change is necessary now; otherwise the WTO mill may come to a total halt.

Section 3

PLAYING ON AN UNEVEN FIELD: The Developing Countries and the WTO/URAs

IS YOUR COUNTRY ALLOWED TO VOTE AT THE WTO?
Yash Tandon

"Is your Country Allowed to Vote at the WTO?" was originally published as the "Director's Comment" in SEATINI Bulletin *Vol 1, No. 2, 30 April 1998. The writer draws on the remarks of World Bank Special Advisor to the WTO, Mr Constantine Michalopoulos, at the first SEATINI Workshop on Strengthening Africa in World Trade in March/April 1998. The comments refer specifically to Eastern and Southern African countries and imply that these countries need to improve their levels of representation and involvement in the WTO.*

The WTO is a member-driven organisation. So, if sufficient African countries get their act together, it is possible to influence the decisions at the WTO. But the only way to achieve this is for African countries to organise themselves and meet the preconditions to participate effectively in the WTO. These are that:

1   A country must be a member of the WTO to be able to vote at WTO meetings; and
2   A country must have paid its membership fee.

If its membership has not been paid for three years consecutively, a country is not able to vote. Not just African countries, but even the US, show some irregularity in their payments but the US has never exceeded the three year limit.

In a snap survey conducted by one of the resource people at the SEATINI Workshop on Strengthening Africa in World Trade (Harare, Zimbabwe, 30 March to 4 April 1998) it was found that, of the eighteen African countries represented at the workshop:

• Two were not members of the WTO at all;
• Five were more than three years behind in the payment of their dues;
• One country was one year behind in its payments; and

- Of those whose payments were up to date, four had no representation in Geneva.

Countries that are more than one year behind in their payments do not receive WTO documents. In addition to not receiving WTO documents, those countries that are three years behind cannot be elected to committees or participate in decisions on the allocation of WTO funds. Thus, of the eighteen countries participating in the SEATINI workshop, twelve could not be effective in the WTO. This left only six countries with some potential for effective participation. But, a country needs at least three people working on WTO matters to be able to cover all the meetings that take place. This was not the case among the remaining six countries. Most of them had only two personnel at their permanent mission to the WTO and these two had to deal to with many other matters besides WTO related ones. This accounts for many of the difficulties that African states have at the WTO and the sample survey quickly conducted at the SEATINI workshop is typical of the general situation of the developing countries in Geneva.

The WTO is too important an organisation to be treated casually. It is not a mere debating society; it is a negotiating forum. The decisions taken within the WTO are contractual and can be enforced through the Organisation's sanctions machinery. It is imperative that African countries treat the WTO with the seriousness that it warrants: become a member; pay your dues; ensure strong representation in Geneva and act in concert with other developing countries.

THE WTO AGREEMENTS: IMPLICATIONS AND IMBALANCES
Bhagirath Lal Das

"The WTO Agreements: Implications and Imbalances" was presented by the author as a paper at the Third World Network Seminar on The WTO and Developing Countries, 10-11 September 1996. Das starts from the assumption that the aim of the Uruguay Round was not to facilitate fair trade but to wring further concessions from the developing countries. Das clearly outlines the imbalances that entered the WTO system at its inception, suggesting possible solutions to each of these. He concludes by warning of attempts by powerful players to further tip the system to their advantage.

One of the main objectives of the proponents of the Uruguay Round was to obtain commitments and concessions from developing countries and it is no surprise that the final result is heavily weighted towards fulfilment of that objective. Consequently, the contents of the agreements have severe imbalances with adverse implications for the interests of developing countries. Hence, an important aim of developing countries in the WTO should naturally be to try to correct these imbalances and make the WTO system more useful to them.

This paper aims to list some of the obvious imbalances that may hinder full utilisation of the system by the developing countries. The listing starts with the mechanism for enforcement of rights and obligations which has been hailed as a big achievement of the Uruguay Round. It then goes on to market access and the systemic issues of contingency actions and further, to sectoral issues and the 'new' areas of services and intellectual property rights. Towards the end, an attempt has been made to list fresh efforts by the developed countries at introducing new imbalances.

Enforcement of Rights and Obligations

Effective enforcement of rights and obligations, through an improved dispute settlement understanding, has been considered to be one of the major achievements of the Uruguay Round. Effectiveness has been enhanced and dilatory tactics have been curtailed by prescribing specific time schedules for various stages of the dispute settlement process and by near automatic establishment of panels and adoption of panel reports.

The process is ideally suited to disputes between partners who are almost equally powerful. The system may prove less effective when a weak trading partner seeks to gain redress against the omissions or commissions of strong trading partners. Some of the general deficiencies of the system, as well as those arising from the weakness of a trading partner are mentioned below:

1   Under normal circumstances a Member with a grievance may have to wait for nearly two years to get any redress. Seven to nine months may pass before the report of the panel or the Appellate Body is available and is adopted. Thereafter, the Member that has been found to have done something wrong will have nearly fifteen months to implement the recommendations fully.

To get full relief in two years after having raised the issue would be considered a case of justice delayed by any standard. Because the resilience of industry and trade in weaker countries is comparatively low, they may not be able to sustain the adverse impact of the wrong action of powerful trading partners for such a long time.

2   Even this delayed relief could be illusory for weak trading partners in some cases. The ultimate means of relief within the WTO framework is through retaliation against the erring trading partner. Normally, of course, the moral and political pressure would work to persuade the erring Member to take corrective action in accordance with the recommendations of the Dispute Settlement Body but, in really difficult cases, where the domestic compulsions of the erring Member render the implementation of the recommendations difficult or inconvenient, it may drag its feet or even totally refuse to take corrective action. Considering the importance of such cases, these may be of great relevance to the affected Member.

In such a situation, the erring Member takes the risk of retaliatory action by the affected Member. Naturally, there will be more willingness to take such risks if the affected Member is not a strong or important trading partner. For an affected developing country it may be difficult, for various reasons, to take retaliatory measures. Politically, it may not be prudent to take action against a strong partner and, economically, retaliation may not be convenient as it also has a cost.

Hence a weak trading partner, particularly a developing country, may sometimes find that the relief through the dispute settlement mechanism is not real or effective.

3   Time limits have been prescribed for the various stages of the dispute settlement process. Obligations in this regard have been laid on the Members and, in some cases, on the panels and the Appellate Body. But, in respect of panels and the Appellate Body, apart from these provisions of time schedules being strongly persuasive and acting as a moral pressure, there is really no relief if these bodies fail to adhere to the schedules.

4   The most serious weakness introduced in the dispute settlement system, and one which has not often been emphasised, is the

severe curtailment of the role of the panels in the disputes relating to anti-dumping. In such cases, the panels have been specifically restrained from pronouncing whether or not a measure is consistent with the obligations of the Member under the Agreement on Anti-dumping. The panels have merely to determine whether the establishment of the facts by the authorities has been proper and whether the evaluation of the facts has been unbiased and objective. Once these conditions have been established, the actual evaluation of the authorities will not be challenged, even if the panel comes to a conclusion different to theirs. Further, if the relevant provisions of the Agreement admit of more than one permissible interpretation, the panels must declare the measure in conformity with the Agreement, if it rests upon one of these permissible interpretations.

The curtailment of the role of panels in anti-dumping cases is particularly harmful to the developing countries as these are the most predominant cases in the disputes involving them.

The decision of the Ministerial Meeting in Marrakesh, says that this provision must be reviewed after a period of three years, with a view to considering the question of whether it is capable of general application. Thus, there is a possibility of this provision being extended to other areas as well. If it actually takes place, it will make the whole dispute settlement process almost totally ineffective.

5   For the past few years, the work of the panels has tended to be intensely technical. They have started going into fine points of law which means that it is becoming difficult for the authorities of developing countries to prepare their cases and make presentations before the panels with their own technical resources. This is particularly so when the other party involved is a developed country and information on details from that country needs to be collected and analysed. Often, the authorities of the developing countries have to employ lawyers and other experts from developed countries which proves very costly. In the case of very poor developing countries, the cost of taking a case to the panels may be totally prohibitive.

These problems suggest their own solutions. For example:

- There should be provision for quicker relief against the encroachment of ones rights by others or failure of other parties to meet their obligations. There should also be provision for compensation to the affected Member, by the erring Member for losses based on the duration for which the measure in question has remained operative. For calculating the quantum of compensation, the duration of the measure causing loss is relevant, rather than the time of initiating the dispute settlement process or the adoption of the panel report. The compensation could be in the form of some trade benefit or even in the form of a cash payment.

- If the erring Member fails to take the corrective action, retaliation should not be left solely to be undertaken by the affected Member. Rather there should be a joint action by all Members. Modalities for this purpose could be worked out. After all, GATT 1994 does provide for joint action by Members in certain circumstances. Alternatively, there could again be provision for financial compensation by the erring Member to the affected Member.

- There should be some built in disincentive for panel members to delay the process beyond the stipulated time limits. For example, one criterion for selecting the panel members could be the timeliness with which they have delivered previous reports.

- The curtailment of the role of the panel in the anti-dumping cases should be completely eliminated and there should be no question of extending this process to any other fields.

- The panels have the discretion to call for materials on their own. There should be a practice that when a developing country party to a dispute makes a case for the need for materials relevant to the case, the panels should collect these materials and take them into consideration. There could also be provision for the panels to award costs to the affected developing countries, to be paid by the erring developed country.

Market Access

It has been repeatedly emphasised that developed countries have reduced their tariffs significantly during the Uruguay Round. They have been credited with having reduced their trade weighted average tariff on industrial products by nearly 39 percent. As a matter of fact, their trade weighted average tariff on industrial products has been reduced from 6.3 percent to 3.9 percent. From the angle of its impact on market access, all it means is that a product with a unit price of $100 will now cost $103.9, whereas it was costing $106.3 earlier.

It is not only the developed countries that have reduced their tariffs. Some developing countries which had very high tariffs earlier, have significantly reduced these. For example, the trade weighted average tariff on industrial products has been reduced from 71.4 percent to 32.4 percent by India, from 40.7 percent to 27 percent by Brazil, from 34.9 percent to 24.9 percent by Chile, from 46.1 percent to 33.7 percent by Mexico, from 50 percent to 31.1 percent by Venezuela, and so on.

In respect of the developed countries, two points have to be particularly noted. First, their average tariff on goods from developing countries is relatively higher than those from developed countries. Besides, their tariffs are relatively high in products of export interest to developing countries, for example, textiles, clothing, leather goods and so on. Second, their tariff escalation continues to be high in spite of the commitments on various occasions to eliminate or reduce it.

The justification often given is that developing countries have, for too long, enjoyed the fruits of the Most Favoured Nation (MFN) treatment given to them by the developed countries. But this is clearly a partial view. It cannot be overlooked that developing countries, in their development process, have absorbed vast quantities of the products of developed countries and have thereby supported their industrial production. This has been particularly evident during the periods of recession in the developed world. Due credit has to be given to developing countries on this account and thus, less attention to products of their interest in the process of tariff reduction in developed countries is not justified.

Instead of putting the developing countries on the defensive in respect of the tariff reduction exercise, developed countries should indeed recognise their contribution and concentrate on further reducing the tariffs on the products of their interest. Besides, there is a need for significantly reducing the tariff escalation in the product chains of interest to developing countries. These countries are fully justified in asking for such action on the part of developed countries.

Contingency Trade Measures

Three areas are covered under this heading, viz, safeguard, subsidies and dumping.

In these areas, significant improvements have been made, particularly by enhancing objectivity and by introducing de minimis clauses. However, it is clear that, in the area of subsidies, it is the developing countries that have made significant concessions. Earlier, their subsidisation was recognised as a tool in their development process. Now, except for a few types of measures like freight subsidy, they are generally debarred from using subsidy as a tool of development.

In these three areas some of the points needing further improvements are listed below:

Safeguard

It is clear that the new Agreement on Safeguard does not permit targeting a country or a set of countries for safeguard action; any such action has to be taken on a global basis. However, in respect of allocation of the share of the global quota, there is a provision for deviation from the normal practice in special circumstances. There is a fear that this enabling provision may be used to reduce the quota of developing countries. Special care needs to be exercised to ensure that this provision is not used in a discriminatory manner, putting developing countries at a disadvantage. One has to be careful with such provisions, particularly in the initial period when practices develop into accepted interpretations. It may be desirable to develop some clear criteria for the conditions and extent of departure from the normal practice of allocation of the share of the global quota.

In safeguard, developing countries have the benefit of some de minimis provisions. However, it is not clear how these will operate. For example, if a Member takes to tariff type measures as safeguard, it is not clear how a developing country falling within the de minimis provision will be excluded from the higher tariff or charge. On the other hand, if quantitative restriction is adopted as a safeguard measure, again it is not clear whether a developing country falling within the de minimis provision will be totally excluded from the restrictions of export of that product into that Member country. Considering that the de minimis provision excludes developing countries falling within such provision from the safeguard action, it is desirable to stipulate clearly that neither the higher tariff nor any limits to export will apply to such countries.

Subsidies

Subsidies which are commonly used in developed countries, for example, those for research and development, for development of comparatively more backward regions and for adoption of environmentally friendly technologies, have all been included on the list of non-actionable subsidies. However, those types of subsidies which developing countries generally apply in the process of industrialisation and development, have generally been excluded.

The industrial and trading firms of developing countries suffer from natural handicaps as, very often, they do not have the advantage of large scale operations, availability of technology and finance, entry into international networking in the relevant sector, and similar other facilities which their competitors in the developed world have. Therefore, it is sometimes necessary for developing countries to provide subsidies to them so that there is diversification and an increase of production and entry into new markets. These needs have been almost totally ignored in the Agreement on Subsidies.

It is necessary to recognise these needs, as was done earlier and as has been done in the case of the subsidy practices of developed countries. Subsidies in developing countries for upgrading and diversification of production, for absorption and adaptation of higher technologies, and for entry into new markets should be treated as non-actionable.

Of course, some special provisions have been made for countries having per capita income up to US$1 000. But, in this case too, some improvements need to be made. For example, a country crossing this limit is excluded from the benefit almost immediately. The rise in income might, in some cases, be a temporary phenomenon and not a structural feature. Hence, there should be a provision for exclusion only when a country has higher per capita income over a period of a few years.

There is a provision for exclusion when a country achieves export competitiveness continuously for two years but there is no provision for automatic inclusion of a country in this category once its per capita income goes down below this critical level. The automatic inclusion should be provided for.

Dumping

The provisions of the Agreement on Anti-dumping have become very complex in the process of using the Agreement, adopting the practices followed by major developed countries in this area. Very often, the calculation of the cost of production and other expenses is involved in preparing the case on either side. For a developing country, it is very difficult to collect this information from developed countries. Neither the authorities nor trade and industry in developing countries are well equipped to locate the sources of such information in developed countries and collect it. Very often the services of law firms of these developed countries have to be employed and it becomes a very costly process.

In fact, considering the vast difference in the resources of the developed countries and developing countries, the process of anti-dumping enquiries, both at the importing end and the exporting end, becomes very much tilted against the developing countries, unless they are prepared to spend enormous amounts on collection of materials from developed countries and engaging law firms from those countries.

The only way out is to have very simple procedures, of course taking care that the process does not become too subjective.

The most serious problem in the area of anti-dumping, is the exclusion of this subject from the normal dispute settlement process, as was explained above while discussing the enforcement of rights and obligations. There is a need to bring this subject into the folds of the common dispute settlement process.

Specific Sectors

Agriculture and Textiles
There has been significant progress in bringing agriculture within the general discipline of GATT 1994. Specific commitments have been undertaken by governments in respect of reducing their import restraints, domestic support and export subsidy. In textiles, an important commitment has been to end the Multi-Fibre Agreement (MFA) with the coming into force of the WTO Agreement and, thereafter, to bring this sector into the fold of the general rules of GATT 1994 by the beginning of 2005. The special arrangement in this sector, in derogation to the general rules of GATT 1994, had continued for nearly a quarter of a century, hence its final demise is an important event in international relations.

However, these two agreements have left in their trail a number of problems. In agriculture, these include:

- Countries which have been maintaining import restraints, domestic support and export subsidy have been obliged to reduce these measures to some extent during the implementation period. Substantial portions of the measures will, however, continue in these countries. But those countries that did not have such measures in the past are prohibited from introducing such measures beyond the de minimis levels. This is patently unfair.

- The agreement is based on the assumption that totally free movement of agricultural products across borders is the most ideal condition. The underlying assumption is that it is desirable for a country to import food from other countries if it is cheap compared to its own cost of production. This principle may perhaps be valid for most of the developed countries which have enough foreign exchange at any time to import whatever they want. But most of the developing countries are short of foreign exchange most of the time. If they depend for their food on import, their population may have to starve at times when they do not have enough foreign exchange to buy food abroad. Such countries may consider it wise to grow their own food as far as possible, even if it is more costly than the food available from some other countries. Food production has many more social and human implications than can be tackled by pure economic considerations. And yet the agreement in this sector aims at abolishing all support for food production and all restraints on the import of food items from outside. This will particularly affect the developing countries with chronic problems of availability of adequate foreign exchange for their imports.

- Another special feature in many developing countries is that agriculture is not considered a commercial activity. Farmers take to agriculture sometimes because they have land and there is nothing else for them to do. For some, it is a purely subsistence exercise. It is extremely difficult to harmonise these special characteristics with the purely commercial and price considerations that are the underlying principles of the current agreement.

- The problems of net food importing countries have been recognised and yet there is no concrete mechanism for tackling this problem in the agreement.

- In the process of tarification, several countries, particularly some major trading countries, have overvalued the tariff equivalents of their non-tariff measures, with the result that their base levels of total tariffs have been recorded as very high.

These problems have to be given serious consideration. Of course, they might be raised during the review process but it may be preferable to start with some of them even before that time.

The main problem in textiles is the process of liberalisation in accordance with the provisions of the Agreement. Several major developed countries claim to have fulfiled their obligation of liberalisation without actually liberalising the items under restraint. They have taken shelter under a strictly technical interpretation of the Agreement without giving any consideration to its spirit. An immediate review of the implementation is needed in order to decide on a revised schedule of liberalisation by major importing developed countries.

Other problems in textiles are that:

- Recent experience has shown that the Textile Monitoring Body (TMB) has not proved all that effective in checking unreasonable use of the transitional safeguard mechanism. In one case, the TMB failed to make its conclusion, even though the Agreement makes it obligatory on this body to give its finding on the measures undertaken by Members and brought before it for examination.

- Generally, GATT 1994 works on the principle of overall balance, but an exception to this principle has found its place in this agreement which has an unusual clause of sectoral balance of rights and obligations.

- Measures in the nature of penalty have been prescribed hitting only developing exporting countries. There is no mention of any explicit penalty for importing developed countries if they fail to abide by their obligations.

Services

The Agreement on Services is basically a framework agreement within which countries undertake obligations for liberalising their service sectors.

One obvious imbalance in this Agreement is the treatment of labour and capital. There is a specific provision allowing cross-border movement of capital, if such movement is an essential part of the market access commitment or if a commercial presence is involved. However, there is no explicit provision on the movement of persons on similar lines.

In respect of developing countries, the agreement makes it clear that their participation in world trade must be facilitated through appropriate negotiated specific commitments. However, in actual practice, this provision has not been much respected. For example, in the negotiations on financial services, some major developed countries insisted on very high levels of commitments from some developing countries which they were in no position to offer.

In fact, the process of sector by sector negotiation is basically flawed because the interests of various countries may not converge in the same sector. The process of give and take would be much smoother if negotiations were undertaken in a large number of sectors at the same time, so that a country is able to offer concessions in some sector for receiving concessions in some other sectors. Based on the difficulties experienced in the sectoral negotiations so far, there is a clear case for rethinking this issue.

TRIPs

The basic imbalance in this Agreement lies in the fact that it provides for minimum protection levels for the holders of intellectual property rights (IPRs). There is hardly any concern explicitly shown in the Agreement for the users of the intellectual property. A balance can be attempted by countries in their legislation within the limits of the discretion allowed in the Agreement.

New Issues

Further imbalances are likely to occur in the WTO Agreements through the introduction of new issues. For example:

- The proposed Agreement on Investment seeks to ensure free entry of investors into a country without any concern for the needs and priorities of host countries;
- Some proposals in the area of environment seek to justify trade restrictions without adequate objective examination in the framework of GATT 1994;

- The proposals on social clauses are thinly veiled attempts to neutralise the advantage of developing countries in respect of their low labour costs, totally forgetting that there is no means of neutralising the advantages of the developed countries in the form of cheaper and easier availability of capital, access to high technology, and highly developed infrastructure and networks;
- The consideration of competition policies may be targeted at clipping the wings of comparatively stronger firms in developing countries so that they do not stand in competition with the well established firms of developed countries; and
- The consideration of corruption may be aimed at attacking the credibility of the authorities and institutions of developing countries.

Conclusion

This illustrative list of problems in the existing agreements in the WTO suggests that the review process in the successive Ministerial meetings for a few years, can remain busy with tackling them and finding solutions. In fact, these and similar relevant problems should be listed and form the agenda for the Ministerial meetings. However, recent experience has shown that these issues of the existing agreements are more likely to be ignored and further fresh issues are likely to keep the Ministerial meetings busy. This trend can be changed only by the concerted action of a group of developing countries that find their interests ignored in the WTO.

INITIAL EUPHORIA OVER WTO GIVES WAY TO REALITY
Chakravarthi Raghavan

"Initial Euphoria over WTO Gives Way to Reality" originally appeared in Third World Economics *No. 189 of 16-31 July 1998. As the title suggests, the writer finds that the WTO has not fulfilled its promise of trade liberalisation and growth in the interests of all member countries. Raghavan highlights a number of measures adopted by the industrialised countries to keep developing country goods, and to some extent services, out of their markets. These include tariff peaks (imposition of heavy tariffs above a certain supply quota), tariff escalation (increases in the percentage tariff rate according to the level*

of processing of imported goods) and, where neither of these is possible, anti-dumping measures against countries supplying goods at less than the price of the same product produced locally.

The initial euphoria over the establishment of the WTO, and the impressive market access achieved by it, has been replaced by the realities faced by developing countries in implementing the obligations and taking advantage of the rights, the UN Economic and Social Council (ECOSOC) was told on 7 July by UNCTAD Secretary General Rubens Ricupero.

While significant barriers to the entry of products of export interest to developing countries remain in place, the ongoing multilateral market access improvements are in areas of export interest primarily to the industrialised countries, raising concerns over the advancement of the legitimate trade and development objectives of developing countries within the WTO framework, he added.

Ricupero was speaking while introducing a joint report on market access prepared by the UNCTAD and WTO Secretariats that showed that significant trade barriers still impede exports of developing countries and that many of their products face tariff peaks and tariff escalation in major trading countries.

The report attempts a 'balancing act' by looking at the tariff and non-tariff barriers in the major Quad countries (Canada, the EC, Japan and the US), which account for nearly 61.3 percent (by value) of world imports of goods, and comparing them with those in South Korea, Malaysia, Brazil (WTO members) and China (which is not even a member). Korea and China account respectively for 2.8 percent and 2.6 percent of world imports, Malaysia for 1.4 percent and Brazil for 1.1 percent. In exports, the Quad account for 71.3 percent of exports, Korea for 2.5 percent, China for 2.9 percent, Malaysia for 1.5 percent and Brazil for 0.9 percent.

The rationale in picking the four 'developing nations' and comparing their tariffs and so on with the Quad's is not clear, except perhaps to show that everyone is guilty of erecting barriers.

A similar balancing act is also found in the comparisons on resort to anti-dumping actions and safeguard measures by comparing actions in the Quad with those in several developing countries.

The report brings out the fact that exports of products of interest to developing countries face tariff peaks and/or tariff escalation in major industrial markets. These cover sectors such as vegetables and fish, food industry products, metals, wood products and furniture, textiles and clothing, footwear, leather and rubber goods, automobiles and other transport equipment and electronics.

The establishment of the WTO and its multilateral trade agreements (MTAs), Ricupero told the ECOSOC earlier, had achieved impressive market access in goods and services, and ensured security of access and a dispute settlement process.

It was noted that clarifications, improvements and monitoring of the MTAs to ensure efficient and effective operation were being undertaken by the WTO committees. The tremendous workload and often tight schedules confirm the belief of WTO members that a balanced, multilateral trade liberalisation process is in the interest of all countries. The WTO serves as a forum for continuous negotiations among members to improve further conditions of market access.

It was not only developing countries that were facing difficulties in implementation, but many developed countries too had been unable to comply with their obligations.

Not Satisfactory At All

Concerns over these difficulties had been underscored at the first and second Ministerial Conferences, and an evaluation has been mandated for the third Ministerial Conference next year, Ricupero told ECOSOC, adding,

> While the implementation of the WTO agreements is on track, we can probably agree that it is not proceeding at a pace and on a scale that is satisfactory to all WTO members. And, without full and faithful implementation, the credibility of the WTO itself may be at stake.
>
> Substantial scope therefore remains for further market access improvement for agricultural and industrial products of export interest to developing countries.
>
> The presence of high tariffs and tariff escalation on products of export interest to low income developing countries, and Least Developed Countries (LDCs) in particular, becomes even more dramatic against the background of ongoing multilateral market access improvements in information technology products, basic telecommunication services and financial services sectors.
>
> These, it should be said, are sectors of export interest primarily to developed countries and a few newly industrialising developing countries. This has, to some extent, raised concerns

among the developing countries over the advancement of their legitimate trade and development objectives within the WTO framework.

A small number of developing countries have succeeded in expanding dynamically their exports of manufactures with middle to high value addition and technological content, including office machines and telecommunications equipment, scientific and controlling equipment, chemicals, electrical machinery and apparatus.

In general, these dynamic sectors face relatively low tariff barriers in the Quad countries as a result of Uruguay Round concessions. The market access improvements under the WTO have contributed to the expansion of the trade of major exporters of relatively sophisticated manufactures among developing countries. However, this increased market penetration by developing countries has resulted in more intense demand from domestic producers in many countries for trade remedies in the form of contingency measures like anti-dumping actions. The most affected sectors include metals, plastics, textiles and clothing, footwear and headwear, Ricupero added,

> Even when duties are ultimately not imposed or are refunded, the actions achieve their intended effect of deterring foreign suppliers from attempting to enter the market by creating uncertainty about market access.

Traditionally, some developed countries have been major users of such non-tariff measures, but some developing countries have also begun to use them with greater intensity, Ricupero added.

In services, the degree of market access commitments under the General Agreement on Trade in Services (GATS) varies considerably among sectors and in relation to particular modes of supply. But considerable scope remains for further liberalisation in a range of service sectors. Progress had been made in negotiations on basic telecom and financial services. But developing country exports of services are hampered by restrictions on temporary movement of persons, particularly economic needs tests, as well as by non-recognition of professional qualifications.

The Uruguay Round had addressed some of the market access concerns of the LDCs, with improvements mainly in the form of duty free MFN treatment for tropical products. Many industrialised countries had also revised their Generalised System of Preferences (GSP) schemes to bring them into line with Uruguay Round requirements to bring substantial benefits for LDCs, though some of their most important exports (including clothing, textiles, leather products, footwear, food and food industry products) continue to face barriers in major markets.

Full implementation of the Plan of Action for LDCs adopted at the Singapore Ministerial Conference was hence a high priority. But most important was to strengthen the supply capacity and competitiveness of these countries in order to maintain their current level of participation in world trade and enable them to exploit the new trading opportunities.

On the preparations for trade negotiations due to begin soon, Ricupero said developing countries need to participate actively and effectively in the ongoing process of implementation of WTO agreements and adequately prepare negotiating agendas to protect their trade and development interests in the forthcoming multilateral negotiating rounds. The developing countries should design a 'positive agenda' to reflect their trade problems and propose concrete negotiating objectives.

UNCTAD, he said, is providing technical support to developing countries in this regard as a matter of priority. But developing countries and their companies need to continue efforts to expand supply capacity and competitiveness to take advantage of market access improvements.

Global Objective

A future multilateral trade initiative should not be simply "a collage" of national or group proposals, but should have a global objective. While some have suggested a target such as global free trade by a certain date, the challenges of globalisation would seem to dictate a more comprehensive approach, a vision of a globalised world where all can enjoy the benefits even though all might not be able to compete in the short run.

"The current Asian financial crisis," he added,

> ...has demonstrated clearly that the international financial system has placed major strains on the international trading system, as the affected countries are having to trade their way out of their financial difficulties. The problems faced in obtaining trade negotiating mandates and the various forms of protest by

those feeling themselves threatened by globalisation suggest that trade liberalisation initiatives should be accompanied by a package of support measures.

For many developing countries, sub-regional agreements that enable them to improve their efficiency and eventually compete in world markets should be encouraged,

But market access must be effectively supported, through well designed policies to increase competitiveness and supply capacity. Thus, investment policy to encourage transfer of technology and channelling of investment into priority areas, the reduction of debt burdens, and trade efficiency measures to streamline trade are vital and deserve the support of the international community.

DEVELOPING COUNTRIES AND NEGOTIATIONS IN THE WTO
Vinod Rege

"Developing Countries and Negotiations in the WTO" was originally published in Third World Economics *No. 191 of 16-31 August 1998 and is extracted from a paper presented by the author at a seminar on the WTO Pre-shipment Inspection Agreement. Within the context of the 'public choice' theory, Rege posits negotiations as a process of interaction between competing interests, rather than a process based on information. Lack of information may arise from: wilful avoidance of the facts, for fear that they my oblige one to change one's point of view; unintentional ignorance (as in the case of many developing countries which do not have the capacity to accurately predict the outcomes of negotiated commitments); or a deliberate attempt to obscure the facts from the other party. As GATT members moved towards the signing of the Marrakesh Agreement establishing the WTO, an example of the last occurred. Developing country members assumed that the WTO would operate on an agreement-by-agreement basis, as the GATT had done, but found at the last moment that they were faced with a 'single undertaking' agreement containing binding provisions in many areas of little relevance to them.*

Trade negotiations in an organisation like the WTO are mainly motivated by two broad objectives:

1   Improvements in access to markets through removal of tariffs and other barriers to trade; and
2   Wherever possible, harmonising rules and regulations which countries apply to goods and services, exported and imported.

Developing countries are generally at a disadvantage in participating in international trade negotiations for varied reasons, including their weaker bargaining position and their inability to carry out technical preparations for participation in such negotiations. These difficulties are more pronounced in the negotiations on rule making because of the more technical and complex nature of the issues discussed.

The Public Choice Approach

Two case studies done under the Commonwealth Secretariat's Technical Assistance Programme, applying a public policy approach to the negotiations (on the Customs Valuation and Pre-Shipment Inspection Agreements), give some insight into the problems and difficulties which developing countries encounter in participating in international trade negotiations on rule making. The public choice approach seeks to analyse the political process, and the interaction between the economy and the political life within the country and relations with other countries, by using tools of neo-classical economic analysis.

The public choice approach proceeds on the basis that there is not one but many actors who influence the negotiating approach that is ultimately adopted by the country in international economic, trade and other negotiations. These include the various sectoral groups which lobby for the protection of their interests, the political leaders who may wish to use the negotiations to fulfil their election promises or to build up their own political future, the bureaucrats who may have an interest in promoting their ministries or, in some cases, their own interests, and lastly the negotiators themselves, who may have their personal axe to grind. This could result in the negotiating approach that is ultimately adopted not always being in the interest of the general public or the consumers who are ultimately expected to benefit from trade negotiations.

Secondly, the public choice approach assumes that these various actors may have differing self interests, but pursue them rationally and in a systematic way to maximise their economic benefits, taking into account the political, institutional and other constraints under which they operate.

Thirdly, it assumes that the various actors who influence the decision making process are not always fully informed on all aspects that the issue under consideration raises and are thus often 'rationally ignorant'. Thus, those who influence the decisions, even though they may act rationally, are not always fully informed on all aspects of the issues under discussion.

In the multilateral trade negotiations on rule making, such rational ignorance on the part of the negotiators may relate to the economic or non-economic factors that make it necessary for the other countries to adopt administrative rules, procedures and practices that are different from their own or to the reasons that make it difficult for them to accept the rules which are proposed as a basis for negotiations.

Overcoming Rational Ignorance

It is, however, always possible for negotiators to overcome their rational ignorance by seeking information, holding consultations on a bilateral basis and, if necessary, making visits to the countries concerned.

The resources and time spent for this purpose are, however, the result of cost-benefit calculations. Negotiators would be more willing to seek the information from countries which are in strong bargaining positions and without whose full support it would be difficult to reach compromise solutions. They may not make the same effort if the countries expressing concerns about the proposed rules are those which, because of the lack of political and economic clout, have weaker bargaining positions and are on the periphery in the negotiating process.

In the Tokyo Round for instance, the EU negotiators were honest enough to recognise that one of the reasons that no progress was being made in the negotiations was their insufficient understanding of the US and Canadian valuation systems. Therefore, they went, at the invitation of the American and Canadian authorities, on a four week study tour to Washington and Ottawa to get first hand information on how the valuation systems of these two countries worked. This helped them in drafting a compromise proposal that was to provide a basis for the Agreement that was ultimately negotiated.

The opposite, however, was noticeable in the attitude of developed countries towards the concerns and problems expressed by developing countries in relation to the Agreement's basic provisions. Developing countries came out of the Tokyo Round negotiations on customs valuation with a great degree of dissatisfaction. In particular, they felt that accession to the Agreement would limit the ability of their customs officials to deal with the cases where goods were deliberately undervalued or overvalued by the importers.

The inability of developed country negotiators to understand and appreciate the reasons advanced by the developing country negotiators for the wide prevalence of valuation malpractices in their countries could, in part, be attributed to the existence of rational ignorance on the part of the developed country negotiator of the economic conditions and the trading environment prevailing in the developing countries, and this provided traders the incentive to indulge in such practices. In hindsight, it would appear that, if the EU officials had also visited the customs services in a few developing countries, there would have been better appreciation of the concerns that were being expressed by the negotiators from those countries.

In the event, it took nearly twelve years of discussions at international level to satisfy the developed country negotiators of the legitimacy of developing country concerns and to secure, in the Uruguay Round of negotiations, acceptance of a solution that would considerably improve the ability of the customs services to deal with valuation malpractices under the provisions of the Agreement.

The 'Veil of Uncertainty'

In the case of negotiators from developing countries, a further handicap arises because of their lack of knowledge of the precise implications for their economies and their trade of the proposals that are under discussion.

The case studies suggest that participants from developing countries may, even during the most crucial stage of the negotiations, remain uncertain of the probable effects on the economy and trade of their countries of the proposed rules i.e. the majority of them participate in multilateral trade negotiations under the 'veil of uncertainty' and not on the basis of 'prism of interest' which assumes that the negotiators are fully aware of the consequences to their economies of the new rules. Such uncertainty often makes them adopt negotiating strategies to 'contain the damage' that they perceive could result from the acceptance of the rules rather than negotiate for the maximisation of benefits to their trade.

Thus (in the customs valuation area), during the Tokyo Round, they tried to contain the damage by negotiating a Protocol that would provide them a grace period of five years after accession to implement the discipline of the Agreement.

Again, in the area of pre-shipment inspections (in the Uruguay Round), their strategy in the negotiations in the final phase was to contain the damage by agreeing to a compromise formulation that they hoped would not require the pre-shipment inspection (PSI) companies to significantly change their existing practices.

The analysis in the case studies brings out three main features of the international trade negotiations held in the past under the GATT. Firstly, because of the hegemony exercised by the two major players, namely the US and the European Union, the agenda for the negotiations, as well as the principles on which the new rules should be based and their content, is largely determined by them.

Secondly, as the subjects for negotiations are brought to organisations like the WTO by these two major players, generally after the preparatory work at inter-ministerial level has been completed and after consultations with concerned national interest groups and discussions with other developed countries have been held in such fora as the OECD, they are far more prepared for discussions and negotiations than the developing countries participating in multilateral negotiations. The latter suffer from further handicaps to participation in such negotiations because:

- Their bureaucrats often lack technical expertise;
- Financial and human resources for the examination and study of subjects that are discussed at international level are limited;
- The mechanism required for inter-departmental cooperation and consultation to identify negotiating interests and to decide on the negotiating approaches is not, as yet, well developed; and
- The various interest groups that, through lobbying, assist and influence governments in determining their policy approaches either do not exist or, where they exist, are not effective.

The influence of these factors on the effectiveness with which different delegations are able to follow their perceived national interests may vary from country to country. As a general proposition, however, it can be said that, as a result of these handicaps, most developing country negotiators remain 'uncertain', during the crucial and even concluding phase of the negotiations, about the benefits that would accrue to their trade and of the economic costs they would have to bear when the proposals under negotiation are accepted and implemented. This uncertainty makes them react to the proposals during the negotiations, with a view only to avoiding the negative effects and containing the damage, rather than negotiating for the maximisation of their economic benefits.

Thirdly, the existence on the part of the negotiators of rational ignorance, particularly of non-economic conditions like trading practices and environment, and the attitude of the people in countries with whom they are negotiating towards abiding by the law, may pose problems of communication and even vitiate the process of negotiations. Such lack of detailed knowledge may be found among negotiators irrespective of the countries they represent. In multilateral trade negotiations, however, the existence of such rational ignorance on the part of negotiators from developed countries mitigates against solutions being adopted that meet fully the concerns expressed by some of the developing countries.

Non-Transparent Negotiations

The case studies further bring out the fact that negotiations are often carried out in small groups and, as such, are not always transparent to those who are not invited to participate.

In the Tokyo Round for instance, the draft text of the Agreement on Customs Valuation was brought to GATT for discussions and negotiations only after tentative agreements had been reached on the main provisions among developed countries. To ensure that such an experience was not repeated in the Uruguay Round, developing countries had pressed for and secured, immediately after the launching of the negotiations, the acceptance of a time framework and programme for work in each of the areas that were selected for the negotiations. The elaboration of such negotiating programmes and other steps taken by the Secretariat went a long way in creating conditions for the improved participation of all countries, particularly of developing countries.

However, during the last crucial and bargaining phase of the negotiations in a number of areas, the negotiations were carried out on an informal basis in small groups. Participation in these meetings was restricted to a limited number of delegations. The other delegations were informed of the progress made in the meetings of such small groups only during periodic formal meetings of the main negotiating groups.

In adopting such procedures, the leading delegations and the Secretariat were influenced by the consideration that the detailed negotiations in most of the areas, like anti-dumping, subsidies and countervailing measures, or in new areas (trade related aspects of intellectual property rights, and trade and services) were becoming highly technical in nature. It was felt that because of their lack of technical expertise, not all delegations would be able to make a useful contribution on all subjects. The delegations were, therefore, encouraged to participate in the negotiations on subjects in which they had vital negotiating interests and also had personnel with the necessary expertise.

The motivation for the adoption of these procedures was, thus, to ensure that purposeful negotiations took place among members who were knowledgeable and appropriately skilled.

In one crucial area, however, the motivation of both the leading delegations and the Secretariat in arranging meetings in a small group was different. This was the area of the negotiations on the institutional framework. The initial negotiations, which ultimately resulted in agreement on the establishment of the World Trade Organisation, were started early in 1990 and were carried out in the first half of the year in absolute secrecy, in meetings arranged over lunches and dinners among a limited group of fourteen or so Ambassadors and which two or three representatives of the Secretariat were invited to attend.

The main reason for those who had taken the initiative for starting the discussions on the subject to keep them secret and confined to a limited number of delegations, representing countries belonging to different regions, was the extremely politically sensitive nature of the proposal. The proposal for the establishment of an international organisation in the trade field, similar to organisations like the IMF and the World Bank in the financial field, had been under discussion at international level for over four decades, with countries holding widely differing views. Public opinion, at least in some countries, was far from favourable. Because of this, those who were initiating the discussions did not desire that the proposal be known to all participants or to the general public until agreements were reached among key delegations representing countries at different stages of development. It was their expectation that, once such agreement was reached among a small group of key delegations on the broad elements of the proposal, it would not be difficult at a later stage to reach consensus in the negotiations on a multilateral basis among all countries. In this, later developments proved them right.

The Secretariat, with its understandable interest in enhancing its own role and improving its image through the transformation of GATT into the WTO, was only too willing to act as a midwife for the birth of the new organisation.

Apart from the establishment of the WTO, the main thrust of the proposal was to ensure that all member countries accepted all of the associated agreements that were negotiated in the Tokyo Round as well as those that would result from the negotiations in the Uruguay Round. Many of the developing countries, which had not acceded to the Tokyo Round agreements, were, however, not fully aware of these proposals that were being considered secretly in the small group.

Throughout the first nine months or so of 1990, developing countries seem to have proceeded on the assumption that they would have an option not to join the Agreement, if they considered that the changes and improvements being negotiated did not meet their expectations and requirements.

It is evident from the case study on customs valuation that these negotiations in the small group were kept secret and most of the developing country participants did not know that acceptance of the agreement would be mandatory for all countries. Likewise, in the negotiations in the area of pre-shipment inspections, the lack of transparency resulted in the delegations from developing countries, who were actively participating in the negotiations, not being aware that they would have to accept the Agreement till only a few months before agreement was reached at the technical level on the outstanding issues.

Pursuing Narrow Interests

The public choice approach is critical of the assumption that nations, while they may consult the various interest groups, base their negotiating policies and approaches on identified national interests and negotiate in international economic and trade conferences with a view to maximising their social welfare. It holds, conversely, that because of the personal perceptions and preferences of bureaucrats, the interests of their political masters and the pressures exerted on them by various interest groups, they may adopt negotiating approaches that serve narrow sectoral or other interests rather than the larger economic and trade interest of the country. It is also common for the ultimate policy approach adopted by a country to be influenced by the perceptions, ideological beliefs, interests and behaviour of the bureaucrats responsible for the policy formulations and of the political masters to whom they report.

Most of the issues discussed in international organisations require inter-departmental cooperation. It is, however, well known that bureaucrats do not always like to cooperate and share work with other departments. They tend, instead, to choose an option that enables them to advance their individual perceptions and the interests of the department where they work in order to control the policy rather than choose the one that would bring the highest benefit to the nation as a whole. And, even within the framework of the policy approach decided at the national level after consultations with the various departments and interest groups, the actual positions taken by the negotiators may be influenced by such factors as their desire to project themselves, to secure recognition and acceptance from fellow delegations or to gain prestige by getting elected as Chairs of the committees.

It has not been possible to analyse the extent to which different interest groups were active at the national level in the examination of the issues that were discussed in the areas of customs valuation and pre-shipment inspections. However, at the international level, the views taken by the International Chamber of Commerce at the various stages of negotiations were to have a significant impact on the attitude taken by the two major players, the United States and the EU, in the negotiations on both these areas.

The policy approach adopted at national level could be influenced by the desire on the part of the negotiators to build up the importance of their department or organisation. For instance, during the Tokyo Round, the decision on the part of the EU negotiators to change their negotiating approach from developing valuation rules based on the Brussels Definition of Value (BDV) in favour of the system that was to be ultimately embodied in the Agreement on Customs Valuation was influenced both by their view that the new system would not only mark an improvement over the BDV system but would also enable the Commission bureaucrats to gain and enhance control over the customs administrations of member states.

The flexibility that national bureaucrats and the actual negotiators have in adopting negotiating approaches on the basis of their personal perceptions and views is greater where the subjects discussed are of a technical nature or relate mainly to administrative rules and procedures that do not raise significant conceptual or policy issues i.e. the subjects are far removed from the attention of interest groups and of the press which could mould the opinion of the general public.

Developing Country Negotiators

In general, it would further appear that the possibility of negotiating approaches being determined on the basis of such personal views and perceptions is far greater in the case of negotiators from developing countries than in the case of their counterparts from developed countries. In a large number of the developing countries, the mechanism for arranging inter-departmental consultations in order to determine the policy approach the country should adopt on the subjects under discussion in international forums has not been well established. Where such a mechanism exists, it is not always used because of inter-departmental rivalries. In most cases, policy is determined by a few bureaucrats from the ministry responsible for representing the country in the relevant international organisation, on the basis of their own assessment of state interest, taking into account, where possible, the views of the foreign ministry and negotiators on the ground. They are able to do this because, in most cases, the industrial and other interest groups whose interests might be affected by new rules and disciplines developed at international level, are not vocal or active in expressing their concerns. Given the magnitude of the economic and social problems which most of these countries face at domestic level, the political parties and general public have also shown little interest in the issues discussed at the international level so far, particularly in the rule making area.

It is not, therefore, unusual for negotiators, at least those from some of the developing countries, to declare proudly that the policy of their governments, on many of the subjects discussed in the international organisations in which they participate, is largely made by them. But, the freedom and autonomy they enjoy also make them more vulnerable to persuasion by the delegations with whom they are negotiating. In reaching compromises on the basis of such persuasion, the possibility of the negotiator's decision being influenced by the interest they have in securing acceptance and recognition and in building up their reputation as an effective diplomat who avoids confrontation and knows when and how to compromise, cannot be entirely ignored.

But the extent to which negotiating approaches are influenced by such personal considerations should not be exaggerated. Most of the negotiators are people of honour, great integrity and intellectual honesty, who abide by basic values and attach the highest importance to their countries' national interests. It would, therefore, be both unrealistic and wrong to hold that, whenever compromises are reached that are not looked upon with favour by the critics, the negotiators must have 'given in' for personal recognition or other advantages. It should be acknowledged that negotiators from developing countries participate in multilateral negotiations on the basis of inadequate knowledge of the economic consequences that the adoption of new rules or the modification of old ones could have on their trade or economies.

The autonomy and the freedom that bureaucrats might have at present are also partly due to a lack of interest on the part of the general public in the economic and trade issues that are discussed at international level. However, recent years have witnessed a trend towards greater interest, on the part of industry and other interest groups as well as the general public in a number of developing countries, in the issues that are discussed in organisations like the WTO.

Under the WTO, all developing countries are required to accept and abide by the obligations that the various WTO legal instruments impose. The flexibility that is available to developing countries in the implementation of some of the obligations under the provisions for special and differential treatment to these countries will gradually disappear. By the year 2005, the WTO legal system will have to be applied by all countries on a uniform basis.

These developments will inevitably lead to the industry and trade sectors and the general public taking an active interest in the activities of the WTO. This, in turn, will gradually make those developing country negotiators who, at present, enjoy a considerable degree of autonomy, reluctant to go by their personal perceptions, views and assessments and encourage them to look for instructions from home, before taking any initiatives.

Apart from national delegations, the other actors who could influence both the process of negotiations and its outcome are the international organisations and the bureaucrats working in these organisations.

Influence of International Organisations

The international organisations help the negotiating process by preparing background documents analysing the various issues under discussion, providing technical assistance to developing countries, and increasingly to the economies in transition, for their improved participation in the negotiations.

However, each international organisation has its own 'ideal', which is determined by the reasons that led to its establishment, its stated objectives and its mandate. Like public interest groups, they pursue policies which, while securing the fulfilment of their objectives, also increase their importance and build up their image. In expressing their views in background documents or in providing technical assistance, the organisations are often constrained by the functional role which the secretariats are expected to perform as well as the political realities under which they operate.

The views taken by international organisations on the subjects under negotiation could, thus, vary because of the different perspectives from which the organisations study and examine the issues.

However, international organisations, by their very nature, cannot act on their own. Their policies are evolved by interaction among three sets of actors:

1   Delegates representing the member states who give broad directions and determine the work programme through meetings of the general assemblies, councils, executive boards and budget committees;
2   The elected head of the organisation and their deputies who provide leadership to the organisation and are responsible for the execution of the work programme; and
3   The professional staff working in these organisations.

The members of professional staff are drawn from different countries and have different cultural backgrounds. But for this difference, their behaviour pattern is similar to that of national bureaucrats. In fact, the public choice approach would suggest that the economic incentives which apply to the behaviour of national bureaucrats also apply to international bureaucrats. Thus, they may show the same reluctance to cooperate with other organisations, or even with their colleagues from the same organisation, as the national delegations show in cooperating with other ministries. Where they have a choice between alternative courses of action, they will ordinarily choose one that gives the organisation or the department in which they work more power and prestige. Like bureaucrats at the national level, they might be also rationally ignorant. Such rational ignorance may relate to the work that other organisations are doing or even to that which other divisions in the same organisation are doing.

Some public choice analysts, however, consider that these characteristics which depict the behaviour of the bureaucrats at national level "are more pronounced in the international than in the national setting". Member states (at international level) are not in a position to exercise direct control on international bureaucrats because the objectives of different member states in relation to the work done by bureaucrats may not be the same and may even conflict.

Political Realities

In theory, international bureaucrats, even those at the middle level (Directors or Chiefs of Division), are considered to have far more discretionary authority and freedom to act on the basis of an objective analysis and assessment of the situation and according to their intellectual persuasion, leanings, beliefs and convictions, than their counterparts in national governments. In practice, however, such freedom of action may be constrained by the political realities surrounding the organisation in which the officials are working. In most organisations, the countries that have economic strength and are politically important exercise disproportionate power and authority. This is so whether the formal decisions are taken by a system of weighted voting, as is the case with organisations like the World Bank and the IMF, or by consensus where decisions are taken on the basis of one country one vote, as in the case of the WTO. In actual practice, the US and the EU, at present, exercise hegemony over the activities in all three of these organisations.

These realities could influence the way the discretion and freedom of action that is available to international officials is actually used by them. They might be more forthcoming when the initiatives taken or actions contemplated are consistent with the policy approaches of the dominant players or conform to the dominant ideology or views prevailing at the time. They would be willing to take initiatives that might not be liked by these players only if, in their judgement, the initiatives taken will at least be tolerated or not objected to by the major players.

Moreover, member states with economic and political strength often use both formal and informal means to ensure that international civil servants exercise discretion in ways that, in their view, are neutral, impartial and responsible. The formal means used include curtailment of financial resources for activities that are considered to be superfluous or not in the national interest. In extreme situations, in order to chastise an organisation, they might threaten to, or even actually, withdraw from the organisation temporarily. Alternatively, they might protest to the management against officials who have taken initiatives that they do not approve of and press for their being shifted from the positions they hold or for their contracts not being renewed.

Most of the studies that have so far been undertaken on the application of the public choice approach to international organisations primarily deal with the behaviour of delegations and its impact on the process and outcome of the negotiations or on the functioning of the international organisation. The few studies that also cover the behaviour of international bureaucrats relate to the functioning of the staff of the IMF and the World Bank. In a recent public choice analysis of the political economy of the IMF, Roland Vaubel[56] observes that the unwillingness of the staff to adopt some of the policy measures that could reduce the rigour of conditions imposed by it in making loans to countries was mainly due to their apprehensions that their acceptance would reduce their 'power' over recipient countries and thus their prestige. The fact that, in most cases, the loan policies and the attached conditions would be supported by the Executive Board, in which developed countries because of the weighted system of voting have a dominant voice, further encourages such behaviour on the part of the staff.

---

[56]Vaubel, R. (1991) *The Political Economy of International Organizations: A Public Choice Approach*, Boulder, CO: Westview Press.

These views differ significantly from the 'dirty work hypothesis' developed in the past by some political analysts, who viewed bureaucrats working in organisations like the World Bank and the IMF as 'selfless' individuals and dedicated internationalists who had nothing but the recipient country's interests in mind.

WTO officials take pride in saying that they are the only international bureaucrats who remain true to the oath to remain neutral which all persons joining the international civil service have to take. They express no views and take no sides. They only prepare factual papers that provide the basis for discussions and reports reflecting the main points made in the discussions. The responsibility for taking views lies entirely with the member states, acting jointly in the meetings of either the Council or the Committees.

Fiction

This, of course, is a fiction; it is promoted because it suits the interests of both the Secretariat and the member states. In practice, as the two case studies show, because of it being a Secretariat of a negotiating body as well as a body responsible for the settlement of disputes, the officials tend to be more cautious and circumspect in expressing opinions and weigh carefully the possible reactions of member states in expressing opinions on subjects on which differences of view exist among member states.

Beyond the findings of the two case studies above, the role which the officials from the secretariats of international organisations should play, and the mechanism that should be adopted for the supervision and control of the discretionary authority available to them, also raise important related questions of personnel policy, particularly in relation to the background and experience of the officer responsible for work, and the steps that may have to be taken, through training, field visits and study tours, to reduce their rational ignorance and to increase their awareness of the political and economic realities in which people in different countries live.

COPING WITH WTO NEEDS NEW INSTITUTIONS IN SOUTH COUNTRIES
Bhagirath Lal Das

"Coping with WTO needs New Institutions in South Countries" originally appeared in Third World Economics *No. 193 of 16-30 September 1998. As is made clear in the previous papers in this volume, the developing countries are not able, within the WTO, to either meet their need for growth and development or even defend the tenuous position they already hold. In light of this, Das suggests that there has been some movement in the balance of power and an increase in the capacity of some of the developing countries. He seeks to back up this small amount of progress with a practical suggestion as to the type of internal institution that might place developing countries in a position from which they could operate more effectively in the WTO.*

Major 'trade' negotiations in some important areas are set to be launched in the WTO at the end of 1999 and the preparatory process for these is most likely to start in the last quarter of 1998. The process of these negotiations and their results will have an important impact on the developing countries and, hence, they need to prepare for it effectively. As in the past, inadequate preparations are most likely to involve grave risks for them.

Ineffective Participation

Experience has shown that developing countries have generally not been effective in the WTO, either in pursuing their own proposals or in defending themselves against the proposals of others. They have succumbed to pressures from the major developed countries and made concessions in the WTO negotiations, without asking for commensurate concessions from them. If this trend continues, the developing countries will lose a great deal in the 1999 process. It is necessary to take corrective steps right now. There may be several reasons why developing countries are facing this adverse situation in the WTO but one major one is that the decision making process in their countries has not kept up with the fast changes in the nature and environment of the negotiations.

There have been two major changes in the nature of these negotiations. First, they have become much more complex. The subjects dealt with have deeper and wider implications for the economy of a nation and, very often, they involve harmonisation of various clashing domestic interests. Second, the role of developing countries has undergone a basic change. In the early phases, they were negotiating to get concessions but now the negotiations are more about getting concessions from them. Such negotiations are naturally much more difficult because one has to find a balance between minimum concessions from one's own side and the maximum satisfaction of the demanders.

The environment in which these negotiations are taking place has also changed significantly. In the 1960s and 1970s, the developed countries had a perception of the role of developing countries as partners in economic progress and growth. The problems of developing countries received sympathetic and serious consideration on the basis of enlightened self interest. But since the mid 1980s, the developed countries have been proceeding with a new confidence in their capacity to solve their economic problems by proper coordination of their own macroeconomic policies. In this respect, the role of the developing countries is seen as very much diminished.

As a result, the problems of the developing countries do not receive the same attention which they used to. They are, at best, seen as minor irritants to be dealt with, as issues at the fringe rather than the centre stage. The enlightened interest of the developed countries has been replaced by apathy and lack of concern. In this new environment, the developing countries naturally have to push very hard to direct the focus towards their problems and the issues of interest to them. All this calls for an effective and strong decision making process in the developing countries. The interests of the country in respect of specific issues have to be identified in a rational and firm way. This will lead to a stronger will to pursue them in any forum. In this process, differing interests among various wings of government and among different interest groups in industry and trade as also between the sectoral interests and the economy as a whole, need to be harmonised, so that the real national interest in respect of any particular issue can be identified.

Differing Interests

For example, at present, generally the subject of international trade, particularly WTO negotiations, is being handled in developing countries in some specific ministries such as, perhaps, the Ministry of

117

Commerce or International Relations or External Affairs. But the complexity of the subjects now having to be addressed makes it difficult for any one ministry to handle them. Often, the implications and even the coverage of the subjects are spread over the jurisdiction of several ministries and they may have differing interests. On a question of liberalising the import of a product, the ministry in charge of the use of the product may favour it, whereas the ministry in charge of its production may have an opposite interest as liberalised imports might have an adverse effect on the domestic industry. Likewise, different sections of trade and industry might have differing, and often clashing, interests on almost every subject relating to the WTO. In the instance cited above, the producer industry of the product whose imports are to be liberalised will be adversely affected, but the user industries or consumers will benefit.

Taking another example, that of liberalisation of the import of financial services, the domestic providers of the financial services may apprehend an adverse effect to themselves, whereas the industry and trade sectors may welcome it as it will widen their choice of sources of such services.

Then we have the new subjects, like investment and competition policy, that are knocking at the doors of the WTO. The impact of multilateral rules on these may be different on different parts of the domestic economy. If foreign investors were given totally free entry into a country, they would naturally like to invest in sectors and areas where they can make quick and high profits with minimum inconvenience. This might prompt the proliferation of consumer industries, like fast food chains, in or around big cities. This will please rich consumers who will have varieties of foreign food to partake of. It might also please the local government because economic activities in the area will be enhanced. But it could have an adverse impact on the economy of the country as a whole since there will be an outflow of foreign exchange through the repatriation of profits, without any commensurate inflow of foreign exchange through such activities.

Similarly, if the proposals regarding high competition standards are made applicable, consumers and big firms may gain as the former will have the opportunity to purchase articles of better quality at lower prices and the latter will have a smaller number of competitors. But the smaller firms may stand to lose as they might find it difficult to compete with big firms. All of this indicates that there is hardly any subject covered by the WTO that does not involve a clash of interests in the domestic economy. Therefore, a comprehensive examination of the issues is required so that the various interests involved are properly weighed and a balanced position is worked out in the best interest of the country as a whole. Then there may also be the need for weighing between the short term and long term interests of the domestic economy.

New Institutional Setup

A comprehensive and detailed examination of the issues has to be undertaken, based on economic and social considerations, keeping in view the differing interests and linkages with different aspects of the economy as also with the overall macroeconomic factors. All this needs serious analytical work based on available and researched information and also wide consultation with different wings of government and the various interest groups and economic operators involved. In several important cases, there may be a need for wide dissemination of information and consultation with different sections of the intelligentsia and the public in general. These tasks are too enormous and complex to be handled by the normal machinery of any particular ministry in any government. They will be much beyond its scope and professional competence.

There is a need, therefore, for a new form of institution in each country to handle these issues and provide input to the decision making process. One such institution could be in the form of a commission comprising one to three members who should be persons of experience, integrity, objectivity and courage, and in whom the government machinery, trade and industry and also the public in general would have confidence. This commission should take up specific issues, examine various aspects, hold wide consultations with relevant persons and interest groups and give its own final recommendation which should form an important input to the consideration of the issues at the decision making level of the government, for example, the Minister, the Council of Ministers, the Cabinet Committee, and so on.

The commission should be independent of, and located outside of any specific ministry, though it could be serviced by the apparatus of a particular ministry. It should have enough funds and resources to conduct a deep examination of the issues, either in house or in specific institutions and universities, for holding wide consultations with the relevant persons and interest groups, and for wide public contact through the media.

119

The subjects of examination could be selected in advance, possibly a particular set of subjects over the space of year, depending on an assessment of the need, and supplemented by ad hoc selection of new subjects on which there is an urgent need for the commission's deliberation. An appropriate mechanism could be worked out for the selection of subjects, either by the ministry handling the subject or else by the commission itself. During the process of negotiations, there may be a need for a continuing examination of the relevant issues that need the approval of the government.

The commission should not be a substitute for the present decision making body or for the normal machinery that advises the decision making body and is responsible for the implementation of government decisions. The commission's role will be to provide independent, objective and substantial input to the decision making process. By the very nature of its composition and functioning, it should carry weight with the decision making authority and should be depended upon for the quality and objectivity of its advice. It will substantially relieve the current machinery which advises the government on policy formulation.

Rational and practical ways can be evolved to ensure smooth interaction between the commission and the current normal machinery, and to remove any potential friction in order to ensure that the two work in full harmony. The current machinery should be responsible for placing the recommendations of the commission before the decision making body. In all likelihood, it will hardly have anything substantial to add to the recommendations. Its own information and other inputs would have been provided to the commission earlier, at the time of examination of the issues, and the commission should have taken this into account.

In matters relating to the negotiations, there will also be a need for proper coordination with the negotiating machinery of the government. The commission would need the input of the negotiators to know the lines of other parties in the negotiations, so as to assess the country's room for manoeuvre. Further, during the process of the negotiations and depending on their progress, there would be a need to work out fallback positions. Here, the negotiating machinery and the commission would have to remain in close touch so that the line of the country in the negotiations evolves depending on the need. Appropriate methods for coordination between the commission and the negotiating machinery will have to be worked out, either in the form of direct contact between the two or through the current normal machinery.

The major benefits expected to flow from the new institutional system, in terms of a systematic and comprehensive examination of the issues from the angle of the interest of the economy as a whole, have been explained above. Besides these, there may be some important strategic benefits as well. A decision taken after such elaborate examination with full transparency and participation of the interest groups and analysts will have a solid foundation nationally. Within the country, it will generate full confidence among the various interest groups, economic operators and the public in general, in the policy decisions of the government. And, of course, its projection and championing outside the country will be strong and convincing. Those responsible for the task will feel fully confident of their stand from the national angle. Besides, this process of decision making will naturally be a safeguard against any softening or weakening of the resolve of negotiating personnel.

The commission type of institution may also be relevant and useful to developing countries in some other areas. For example, similar special features exist in the areas of industrial policies and even macroeconomic policies, and a commission in each of these areas could provide substantial input to the decision making process.

STRENGTHENING AFRICA IN WORLD TRADE: RECOMMENDATIONS OF THE 1ST SEATINI WORKSHOP ON STRENGTHENING AFRICA IN WORLD TRADE 30 March to 4 April 1998

The Southern and Eastern African Trade Information and Negotiations Institute (SEATINI) began its life in 1998 (as and 'Initiative' rather than an 'Institute') with a series of sub-regional workshops on Strengthening Africa in World Trade. The participants were African trade negotiators while the resource people were experts (many of whom are contributors to this volume), mainly from Africa and Asia. Participants were given extensive background to the GATT/WTO as well as detailed explanations of the constraints that developing, and particularly African, countries face within this system. Wherever possible, the resource people offered solutions or suggestions on the way forward. "Recommendations of the 1st SEATINI Workshop on Strengthening

121

Africa in World Trade", a summary report of the workshop findings, was prepared during the course of the workshop by a participants' drafting committee.

1   Introduction

The Southern and Eastern African Trade Information and Negotiations Initiative (SEATINI) Workshop was held in Harare from 30 March to 4 April under the auspices of the International South Group Network (ISGN). It was facilitated by resource persons with wide experience in international trade issues.

The Workshop, which was aimed at initiating a process of strengthening the capacity of African trade negotiators, was attended by senior trade negotiators from seventeen Eastern and Southern African (ESA) countries. Other participants were from non-governmental organisations (NGOs) as well as civil society.

The Honourable Nathan Shamuyarira, MP, Minister of Industry and Commerce, Zimbabwe officially opened the Workshop.

2   Deliberations

The Workshop reviewed the participation of ESA countries in the WTO and, in particular, addressed the following key issues:

1   The performance of the developing countries, and of African Countries in particular, in the WTO;
2   The role of regional integration for strategic engagement with the WTO, including the performance of African countries under the Lomé Convention;
3   The Built In Agenda and New Issues emerging at the WTO; and
4   The implications of the implementation of the WTO Agreements for the developmental prospects of African countries.

2.1   Performance of African Countries in the Multilateral Trading System

The multilateral trading system (MTS) has assumed increasing importance in the economies of all countries. Despite this, the participation of African countries in the WTO has been disappointing, principally because:

- African countries have merely been reacting to the proposals and initiatives of the developed countries;

- There is a general lack of coherent national trade policies in ESA countries;

- The countries lack the human and institutional capacity to understand, negotiate and implement WTO Agreements;

- There is no effective consultative mechanism for ESA countries at national or regional levels; and

- Staffing in the missions of the ESA countries represented in Geneva is inadequate.

2.2   Regional Integration and Participation in Lomé

Regional integration within African countries is recognised as an important strategic base for African countries to:

- Negotiate, amongst themselves, appropriate frameworks for cooperation and coordination towards more balanced and mutually beneficial relations between countries at different levels of development;

- Develop and diversify their productive capacities through combined and complementary programmes to improve their productivity and export capacities both before and as they seek to enter more competitively into the global economy; and

- Create a collective base for African countries to engage more effectively in the multilateral negotiating processes that are shaping the terms for international trade, investment and other trade related issues in the WTO.

The Workshop noted that there were several regional trading arrangements in eastern and Southern Africa that could be used as a means to develop and integrate the ESA economies more effectively into the global economic system. The processes in the WTO should not hamper the regional arrangements to which developing countries belong.

With respect to Lomé, the Workshop noted that the ESA countries had not benefited much from the preferential arrangements under Lomé due to restrictions arising from the use of the rules of origin, safeguard provisions and high tariffs on specific agricultural products, and bureaucratic delays in implementing the benefits from the arrangement. The Workshop also noted that the main thrust of the EU Green Paper on the future Lomé is on reciprocal preferences. It was observed that the EU has already prepared its negotiating mandate. This mandate aims, among other things, to use a future ACP-EU cooperation agreement to enforce a narrow implementation of existing WTO rules and agreements on services, investment and intellectual property, and to promote the adoption of new rules on investment, competition, and procurement, to the detriment of the developmental needs of ESA countries.

2.3   Built In Agenda and 'New Issues'
The Workshop noted that:

- Many of the UR Agreements set varying timetables for future work in the WTO which include new negotiations in some sectors, timed reviews in others and assessments of the situation in yet other sectors;

- The Working Groups on the 'new' issues (Trade and Competition Policy, Trade and Investment, and Transparency in Government Procurement) were established predominantly at the insistence of developed countries and have started their work. A Committee on Trade and the Environment has been considering the linkage between trade and environment

2.4   Implementation and Implications
The Workshop noted that the burden of implementation of Uruguay Round (UR) commitments is rather heavy. The UR Agreements are very specific about the timing of the implementation of various obligations. The implementation has four broad elements:

1   Formulation of laws, regulations and procedures to give effect to the Agreements;
2   Establishment of new institutions;
3   Elimination of trade measures that conflict with the URA within a given timeframe; and
4   Sending in and complying with the notification requirements of the Agreements.

The Workshop identified some of the problems and constraints affecting the implementation of multilateral trade agreements that should form a basis for a future WTO negotiation agenda, notably:

- The difficulties in complying with the heavy burden of notification requirements;

- The manner in which most developed countries are implementing their obligations under the UR Agreements which leaves a lot to be desired, eg. increased resort to SPSs, TBT measures and other NTBs, which result in a lack of any real opening of trade opportunities;

- The need to formulate and introduce laws, regulations and procedures for the implementation of some of the agreements, which can be very expensive;

- The lack of provisions that focus on enhancing the supply side capacity of ESA countries, particularly as it was noted that existing market access provisions are insufficient; and

- The imbalances in certain agreements which require rectification (eg. TRIMs, the Agreement on Agriculture and the Subsidies Agreement), including restitution of lost rights.

3   Recommendations

African countries should be proactive and better prepared for WTO negotiations, especially in possible new areas. This could be achieved, *inter alia*, through defining their trade related objectives and needs in order to identify the issues of interest to them. On this basis, they could proceed to strategically determine the most appropriate negotiating strategy.

3.1   Strategies for New WTO Negotiations 2000 and Beyond

The Workshop noted that opinion is divided on starting a new round of trade negotiations, a new round with a sectoral approach and negotiating within the context of the present round. Proponents of each argument acknowledge two basic approaches, namely:

1   Built In Agenda, or
2   Built In Agenda plus New Issues.

The Workshop strongly opposed the idea of a new round and recommended that negotiations on the Built In Agenda continue within the context of the present round but should the agenda overlap with new issues, ESA countries should be prepared to formulate new issues of interest to them for inclusion in the new negotiations, to be undertaken on a non-sectoral basis.

The Workshop recommended that the developed countries' Uruguay Round Agreements (URA) commitments be fully implemented, particularly the WTO Ministerial decision on measures concerning the possible negative effects of the reform programme on least developed countries and net food importing countries.

Developed countries should be urged not to use some of the multilateral agreements, in particular, the Anti-Dumping Agreement and, the Sanitary and Phytosanitary and Technical Barriers to Trade Agreements, in a discriminatory manner that creates barriers against imports from developing countries.

With respect to the Built In Agenda, the following recommendations emerged:

3.1.1 *Market Access*
Whenever there is injury or threat of injury to their domestic industry, ESA countries should take safeguard action. Whenever there is injury from dumping, there should be anti dumping action. ESA Countries should establish appropriate mechanisms for these purposes.

ESA countries ought to ensure that future multilateral trade negotiations take into account their developmental needs. In this regard, African countries are urged to take up issues affecting the entry of their products into the developed country markets, in WTO including:

- Tariff peaks and tariff escalation targeting particular sectors of export interest to ESA countries; and
- Non-tariff measures, particularly Sanitary and Phytosanitary measures.

3.1.2 *Agriculture*
It was noted that some African countries, at the time of entry into force of the Agreement on Agriculture, had either not notified their existing subsidies or notified that they had no subsidies and had thus, unwittingly, forfeited their right to maintain or introduce subsidies. This is an issue which needs rectification in order to enhance flexibility for

African countries in the use of measures to stimulate agricultural production and exports.

It is, therefore, recommended that positive steps be taken to rectify certain anomalies with respect to the application and operation of existing 'standstill' commitments on domestic support and export subsidies under the Agreement on Agriculture. With respect to the elimination of trade measures within a specified timeframe, it was recommended that ESA countries urge a review of the 'standstill' commitment on domestic support and export subsidies under the Agreement on Agriculture.

3.1.3 *Services*

African countries are encouraged to study their services schedules, particularly when the GATS Agreement comes up for review in 1999/2000. Developing countries should push for the consolidation of their rights under the GATS Agreement, in particular:

- The right not to be compelled to afford reciprocity to the developed countries; and
- The right to the use of safeguard action.

ESA Countries should be aware that they are currently under no obligation to liberalise, or they may liberalise only a few sectors. In the Services sectors due for review, developing countries should selectively consider the sectors to be liberalised.

3.1.4 *TRIPS*

The Workshop noted with concern that the overall implications of the Trade Related Intellectual Property Rights (TRIPs) Agreement is that it would have a serious negative effect on development; especially on the capacity and opportunities for developing countries to develop and use indigenous and local technologies. In implementing the TRIPS Agreement, ESA countries should be aware that there are various options in each of the aspects of TRIPS and they should identify and choose the options that are most appropriate to their interests and least damaging.

Moreover, ESA countries should begin the process of proposing changes in the TRIPS Agreement that would be in their interests and in the interests of development.

In view of its adverse implications for development, ESA countries should carefully examine many aspects of the TRIPS Agreement in order to be prepared to propose appropriate amendments during the review process.

The ESA countries should urge that the TRIPS Agreement prohibit the patenting of biological materials and living organisms (whether naturally occurring or modified), as this patenting would have adverse effects on community rights. In the event that this proposal is not accepted, a fallback position of effectively protecting community rights should be advanced. This would include ESA countries establishing a *sui generis* system that protects the intellectual rights and knowledge of communities in relation to plant varieties. The Workshop endorsed the OAU/STRC Task Force declaration on community rights and access to biological resources and the related draft legislation and urged OAU governments and ministers to take measures to implement these in their national policies.

ESA countries should actively participate in the Convention on Biological Diversity (CBD) to establish an equitable system of the sharing of benefits in the use of biological resources and to ensure that the treatment of IPRs does not facilitate biopiracy but, instead, prohibits it and protects the rights of local communities and developing countries.

3.1.5 *TRIMs*

African countries are facing serious problems in conforming to the Trade Related Investment Measures (TRIMs) Agreement as it places serious constraints on their industrial development. Under the TRIMs Agreement, it is recommended that a review of the National Treatment requirement (Article 2) be undertaken as a matter of priority, (insofar as the domestic content requirement which was of immense benefit to ESA states has been explicitly prohibited by Article 2.2). This prohibition results in an unnecessary outflow of foreign exchange from ESA states.

3.2 New Issues

With respect to new issues, the following recommendations emerged:

3.2.1 *Trade and Investment*

The ESA Countries, should ensure that they put forth their views effectively in promoting development perspectives and principles in the process of the work of the WTO working group.

ESA countries should note with great concern that the objective of the industrialised countries pursuing the subject of investment policy in the WTO has been to work out a multilateral framework or agreement within the WTO to curtail the rights and discretion of the host countries to regulate the inflow, conditions and operations of foreign investment in order to provide full freedom and rights for the foreign investors. The ESA countries have to remain fully prepared to meet with the situation when the developed countries come back with their old proposals. Therefore, the ESA countries should start considering the various elements from their point of view to ensure preparedness during the envisaged review of the TRIMs in 1999.

The ESA countries should continue to regulate and welcome foreign direct investment (FDI) with caution. These countries should oppose any proposal that might be brought into the WTO regarding the Multilateral Agreement on Investment (MAI). Instead of negotiating an MAI, taking into account problems of developing countries, the ESA countries should advocate that negotiations start on liberalisation of labour movement.

The OECD countries may complete their Multilateral Agreement on Investment and then pressurise developing countries to join. As the MAI removes the rights and discretion of developing countries to regulate foreign investors, and as its dispute settlement system is of grave concern, ESA Countries should reject any attempts to get them to join the MAI.

3.2.2 *Government Procurement*

The working group in the WTO is undertaking a study on transparency in government procurement practices with a view to developing elements for an appropriate agreement on this subject. The ESA countries should:

- Effectively participate in the working group and, in so doing, be careful that they do not take unreasonably heavy obligations on themselves; and
- Recognise with concern that this study is an initial and interim exercise by industrialised countries with the further aim of bringing in proposals to expand the markets for their goods through the introduction of the principles of MFN and National Treatment in Government Procurement.

The ESA Countries should guard against such a move. Africa should realise that the exclusion of Government Procurement from the principle of National Treatment is a part of the existing rights and obligations (under Article 3.8(a) of GATT 1994) and it is beneficial to them.

3.2.3 Competition Policy

At the first WTO Ministerial Meeting in Singapore, the Ministers agreed to:

Establish a working group to study the issues raised by Members relating to the interaction between trade and competition policy, including anti-competitive practices, in order to identify any areas that may merit further consideration in the WTO framework.

The Workshop noted with concern that, with the introduction of competition policy, which was being spearheaded by the major players, the aim was for these powers to get to the south and establish 'effective' domestic anti-monopoly laws so their corporations can have better market access. Whilst developing countries may decide themselves that they require competition policy, they must beware of proposals that pressurise them to have laws that inadvertently pave the way for big foreign firms to take over and monopolise their economies.

The workshop observed that, although the work of the working party was not over yet, the developing countries needed to introduce disciplines on foreign firms so that domestic consumers did not suffer and domestic producers and traders had necessary safeguards. There was also a need for a multilateral framework for eliminating or curbing anti-competitive practices in international trade. Similarly, mergers of very big firms, leading to significant constraints on competition in international trade, should also be put under some discipline. Specific obligations of the firms in home countries should be defined and enforced.

The workshop recommended that African governments should effectively participate in the working group on competition to protect their interests, including calling for a review of the impact of trade liberalisation on competition in international markets.

3.3 The Performance of African Countries in the WTO

The ESA countries should define their national and regional development objectives from which they would elaborate trade strategies that contribute to the achievement of long term sustainable and equitable development. In addition the workshop recommends that:

- There be effective allocation of human resource capacities by African countries in their WTO missions in Geneva. It was noted with concern that more than twenty African Countries are not represented in Geneva. ESA missions in Geneva need to be strengthened both quantitatively and qualitatively by skilled persons.

- At the regional level, the SEATINI could be encouraged to become a consultative mechanism for government officials and civil society on trade and trade related matters for strengthening the enabling institutions and systems that support the capacities of African businesses to trade.

- The ESA countries should strengthen their institutional capacity to participate effectively in international trade and in the activities of the WTO. To achieve this, these countries should increase their representation in Geneva and Brussels. The strengthened institutional capacity should be complemented with extensive coordination both in and between Geneva and the Capitals.

- The ESA countries should explain their positions firmly, clearly and boldly in the formal and informal meetings in the WTO. Mutual support amongst African and other developing countries would help this process.

- The ESA countries should urge all developing countries to give special support to the interests and positions of the least developed countries in the WTO.

- The ESA countries, on reporting back on the outcome of the High Level Meeting (HLM), should emphasise the need to address supply side constraints. This is important if these countries are to benefit from the market access pledges. There is a need to ensure that these market pledges are notified. There should be a well defined process of co ordination among the six agencies and with the participating least developed countries on the implementation of the Integrated Framework.

- The ESA countries should press for more firm support on the question of debt relief if the LDCs are to be effectively integrated into the trading framework. The participation of the six agencies in the Integrated Framework for LDCs provides a forum at which these important issues of debt can be tackled. The impact of debt on trade should not be overlooked.

- Countries that did not make commitments for improved market access conditions in favour of LDCs in the High Level Meeting should be encouraged to do so, in light of deficiencies in the capacity of developing countries in the region to participate effectively in the WTO, and to establish integrated programmes of technical assistance and institutional support that include all countries, not only the least developed.

- ESA countries should urge coordination between the World Bank, IMF and WTO in order to avoid contradictions in the commitments, as well as implementation, of their programmes.

3.4   Regional Integration and Participation in Lomé

The Workshop noted that integration into the international trading system was a function of a country's ability to:

- Identify and exploit trading opportunities;
- Effectively defend its trading rights;
- Fulfil its trade obligations; and
- Define and pursue its trade and development interests in trade negotiations.

The Workshop appreciated the fact that the ESA countries had individually and/or collectively elected to identify themselves with the existing regional integration arrangements or groupings, eg. COMESA, SADC, IGAD, etc., as a basis for development and engaging more competitively in global trade. It was noted that such initiatives could also promote further trade liberalisation and may assist least developed and developing countries to integrate more effectively into the international trading system.

The Workshop noted the importance of the existing regional arrangements involving the EU and ACP countries and recommended that:

- The starting point for future EU-ACP trade negotiations should be a firm commitment from the EU to maintaining the existing preferences currently granted in ACP countries. Without such a commitment, the very real danger exists that the debate around future relations could generate a level of uncertainty which could have serious consequences for investment and production in key areas of ACP economies (eg. textiles, fisheries, agro processing, horticulture, floriculture, etc.). It was the Workshop's strong view that, from this starting point, consideration should be given to enhancing existing preferences in those areas where ACP economies can gain immediate benefit and such action wouldn't pose any real threat to domestic EU industries.

- A future framework of cooperation must support ACP countries in rectifying the imbalances contained in the rules and agreements of the WTO and prevent the adoption of further rules that undermine the needs and interests of ACP countries.

- It is essential that any external support for the regional groupings in ESA should take into account the different levels of economic, administrative, institutional and political development of these countries in order to ensure that the processes of integration are politically, economically and socially sustainable.

It is also vital that the pace, extent and structure of moves towards closer regional integration are determined with a view to ensuring an equitable distribution of benefits and costs. This is particularly important where there are vast differences between the levels of development of the countries concerned.

GLOSSARY OF ACRONYMS AND TERMS
USED IN THE TEXT

ACP	Africa, Caribbean and Pacific - a grouping of developing nations from these regions, defined specifically by their relationship to the European Union
Anti-Dumping	Measures taken by a country to prevent the import of goods produced more cheaply in another country than they are produced locally
Appellate Body	The legal body overseeing the application of the WTO Dispute Settlement Understanding (DSU)
ASEAN	Association of South East Asian Nations
BBC	British Broadcasting Corporation
BDV	Brussels Definition of Value - the price which the goods would fetch on sale in the open market between a buyer and a seller independent of each other, established by comparing the seller's invoice price with the prices at which identical or similar goods are sold or offered for sale to the country of importation
BoP	Balance of Payments
Bretton Woods Agreement	The 1947 agreement establishing the International Monetary Fund and the International Bank for Reconstruction and Development (World Bank)
Built in Agenda	Negotiations on Services, Agriculture and Textiles mandated in the text of the WTO Agreements
CBD	Convention on Biological Diversity (1992)
CFC	Common Fund for Commodities
COMESA	Common Market for Eastern and Southern Africa
DS	Dispute Settlement system of the World Trade Organisation
DSB	Dispute Settlement Body of the World Trade Organisation
DSU	Dispute Settlement Understanding of the World Trade Organisation
ECOSOC	Economic and Social Council of the United Nations
EEC	European Economic Community
ESA	Eastern and Southern Africa
EU	European Union

UNESCO	United Nations Educational, Cultural and Scientific Organisation
UNIDO	United Nations Industrial Development Organisation
UR	Uruguay Round of trade negotiations held from 1986 to 1994 and concluded in the Marrakesh Agreement of 1994
URA	Uruguay Round Agreements
US	United States
USA	United States of America
VER	Voluntary Export Restraint
WHO	World Health Organisation of the United Nations
WTO	World Trade Organisation